Keto Baking

2 Manuscripts:

Keto Bread and Keto Desserts

Richard Miller

Book I: Keto Bread

Table of contents

Introduction

This guideline for Keto Bread will provide a new way of eating your favorite bread products. You will also learn how to prepare bread – the 'ins' and 'outs' of it all. The following chapters will discuss how to follow the ketogenic techniques combined with your new bread recipes can provide you with healthier choices. Now a brief history of the ketogenic plan and how it works.

During the Paleogenic period, humans were known to hunt for their protein and gather their vegetables, fruits, nuts, and seeds to survive. Because this method isn't ideal in today's society; you don't have to search for food each day. That was the way people lived centuries ago which made the body develop a survival mechanism to survive during times when food was scarce.

Whenever a person encountered satiation where they consumed more calories than they burned, the unused calories would be converted into fat fuels and stored for emergency starvation times. This mechanism was useful in times where nutrient resources were scarce and required a lot more energy to locate.

However, in modern times, food is not only natural to come by, but most meals that are affordable are packed full of unnecessary calories. Our bodies continue to create these fat stores, even though the times of hunting and gathering are behind us. These facts were taken into consideration when the ketogenic diet was developed.

The ketogenic diet or keto diet plan is a low-carbohydrate and high-fat system. It provides satisfactory levels of protein which is similar to other low-carbohydrate diets. It has been called many names including a keto diet, ketogenic diet, low-carb diet, or a low-carb & high-fat (LCHF) diet.

Ketosis is a process that occurs every day, no matter what or how many carbs you consume. The superior keto plan speeds up the process with a standard and safe chemical reaction. The methods used will reduce your body's carbohydrate intake drastically as it is replaced with fat. Your body goes into ketosis which is a metabolic state making your body burn fat for energy. Your brain can also receive energy—transported as ketones from the liver when fat is exchanged. Your body produces insulin and blood sugar/glucose when you eat foods high in carbohydrates; which as a result, are also lowered on the ketogenic diet.

The plan maintains adequate amounts of protein, so your body can repair and regain a healthy status. The diet will also supply you with the calories needed to keep a healthy weight for your height and age.

I hope you enjoy each of the informative segments in your new book of Keto Bread. The nutrients have been calculated for your convenience including the net carbs, protein, calories, and total fats. The calculations may vary, but you will find a ton of useful information; please enjoy!

Chapter 1: Bread Baking: The Basics

Stages of bread baking are in existence when you prepare to bake and carry out the entire process of bread baking.

This is a short guideline of the procedures used throughout this publication.

Mix the Raw Ingredients: In the case of bread, most of your raw ingredients consist mainly of water, yeast, salt, and flour. Then, you just combine them into the dough.

Sift the Flour – Or Not: If you take a page out of Grandma's book and sift the flour, it will aerate and remove any lumps from unsifted flour. The sifted flour is much lighter and is enriched with oxygen - making it easier to mix with other fixings - as you prepare the dough. After the flour is sifted, it is more likely to have an accurate measurement. When possible, always sift the flour.

Proof and Shape the Bread: The proofing phase of baking is where the yeast eats the sugars out of the flour. The result is that it burps out gas and alcohol. As a result, the bread will rise to provide a natural - sweet flavor.

Baking the Bread: Baking is considered the stage where you apply the hot oven to your masterpiece. You will be creating a tasty and delicious treat.

Baking Your Bread At Home: you are 'proofing' and nurturing the dough so you can prepare a healthy meal for your family. Your primary goal is to achieve a tasty loaf of bread that both looks and tastes like it came from a professional bakery.

Store Your Bread to Enjoy Any Time: The final phase is the easiest, just enjoy the bread.

How Much to Knead:

The most logical clue to when the dough has been kneaded enough is that you are tired. That conclusion and the following factors will let you know when enough is enough:

- **The Dough Holds Its Shape:** Once the kneading is successful, you can hold the bread in the air, and it will maintain its form. The ball shape means the gluten is 'strong' and tight.

- **The Dough Is Smooth:** You will start noticing a lumpy – shaggy mass forming as you knead. The mixture should be just slightly tacky when touched.

- **Perform the Poke Test:** Go ahead, and poke the mixture. If the hole fills in quickly, it's ready.

- **Perform A Windowpane Test:** Pull a portion of dough (tennis-ball size). Stretch it paper-thin. If it holds together, it's ready to bake.

The 'true' point of kneading the dough is to strengthen the gluten (the stringy protein bands that provide texture to the bread. As a rule-of-thumb, it should take 8-10 minutes using a mixer or 10-12 minutes is working the dough by hand.

When Bread Is Done:

- **Tap the Bottom of the Baking Pan:** This is a simple process. You take the pan out of the oven and turn it upside down on a flat surface. Tap the bottom, and it should sound hollow when the bread is done. Towards the end of the baking cycle, you can try this method every 5 minutes.

- **Visually Gauge the Doneness:** With experience, you will learn how the bread's appearance changes during the cooking cycle. The color should be a deep golden brown and firm. Don't worry about the darker spots here-and-there; it's normal for home-baked bread.

- **Check the Bread Internal Temperature:** Gently insert the thermometer into the center of the loaf of bread. Most bread is baked at 190°F. Once you add eggs, butter, or milk, the temperature averages 200°F.

Useful Tools & Equipment:

- **Tool 1: Scales:** Portion control is essential for baking bread. You want a scale that will accommodate your needs. Consider these options:
  - **Seek a Conversion Button:** You need to know how to convert measurements into grams since not all recipes have them listed. The grams keep the system in complete harmony.

  - **Removable Plate:** Keep the germs off the scale by removing the plate. Be sure it will come off to eliminate the bacterial buildup.

o **The Tare Function:** When you set a bowl on the scale, the feature will allow you to reset the scale back to zero (0).

- **Tool 2**: **Accurate Measuring Tools:** A measuring cup and spoon system that shows both the Metric and US standards of weight is essential, so there is no confusion during prep.

- **Tool 3: Food Processor, Immersion Blender or Regular Blender**: Each of these will be an essential part of preparing many of the recipes for desserts.

- **Tool 4: Instant Read Thermometer**: You can take out the guesswork if you use a handy 'basic' thermometer.

- **Tool 5: Sifter:** Purchase a good sifter for under $10, and you will be ensured a more accurate measurement for your baking needs.

- **Tool 6: The Mixing Bowl or Tub**: If you are stocking your kitchen for baking, it's essential to choose a clear container where you can see the contents of the bread process.

- **Parchment Paper** will be used for most of the bread recipes. The baking pans are lined with the paper, and the baked goods do not stick. For most baking needs, you can omit the oils if you choose the paper instead.

Chapter 2: The Ketogenic Basics

Learning how to eat healthier just takes patience and practice. You incorporate many of the healthier choices as you bake your delicious bread, breadsticks, muffins, and so many more delicious treats using your ketogenic techniques. First, you need to understand how the macronutrients are calculated.

Everyone's totals are different since your percentages are calculated according to your weight, age, gender, body fat percentage, and activity levels. You can go online and type in *MyFitnessPal, Ruled Me,* or other sites and use the keywords *'keto macro calculator'* to locate the scale guideline. Just type in your information, and it will provide you with your macro limits. Devise a method that works for you. Once you have the numbers, you are ready to begin your journey through ketosis.

In case you don't know, macronutrients are building blocks of food consisting of fat, protein, and carbs. For a regular American diet, you may have a diet composed of 16% protein, 34% of calories from fat, and approximately 50% of the calories from carbs. The ketogenic technique mixes it up with about 25% protein, 70% fat, and 5% from carbohydrates. However, this is not a perfected science, but these are the averages of calculation. Don't worry, because each of our recipes has the essential information as your guideline to ensure you don't overeat.

Make Healthier Choices

Eliminate or Avoid Added Sugars:

- **Stevia Drops** include hazelnut, vanilla, English toffee, and chocolate flavors. Stevia is a common herb known as sugar leaf and is available in drops, glycerite, or in powder form. Enjoy making a satisfying cup of sweetened coffee or other favorite drink. Some individuals think the stevia drops are too bitter. At first, use only three drops to equal one teaspoon of sugar.

- **Xylitol** is at the top of the sugary list. It tastes just like sugar! The natural occurring sugar alcohol has the Glycemic index (GI) standing of 13. If you have tried others and weren't satisfied, this might be for you. Xylitol is also known to keep mouth bacteria in check which goes a long way to protect your dental health. The ingredient is commonly found in chewing gum. Unfortunately, if used in large amounts, it can cause diarrhea - making chewing gum a laxative if used in large quantities. *Pet Warning*: If you have a puppy in the house, be sure to use caution since it is toxic to dogs (even small amounts).

- **Swerve Granular Sweetener** is also an excellent choice as a blend. It's made from non-digestible carbs sourced from starchy root veggies and select fruits. Start with 3/4 of a teaspoon for every one of sugar. Increase the portion to your liking. Swerve also has its own confectioners or powdered sugar for your baking needs. On the downside, it is more expensive.

- **Pyure's Organic All-Purpose Blend** is considered the best all-around sweetener. Many who use it believe it has less of a bitter aftertaste versus a stevia-based product. The blend of stevia and erythritol is an

13

excellent alternative to baking, sweetening desserts, and various cooking needs. The substitution ratio is one teaspoon of sugar for each one-third teaspoon of Pyure. Add slowly and adjust to your taste since you can always add a bit more.

Note: If you need powdered sugar, just grind the Pyure sweetener in a NutriBullet or high-speed blender until it's very dry.

- **Sorbitol** is a sugar alcohol manufactured from cornstarch which can be used in powder form to withstand high temperatures.

- **Coconut sugar** is much lower than table sugar with 15 calories or 4 grams of carbs per teaspoon.

The list of sweeteners listed has a glycemic index rating next to them. This is a measurement of how much your blood sugar is raised after you consume a specific food. If there is a zero (0) next to it; that means it will not increase your blood sugar counts. The measurement can reach 100 which is the baseline of insulin.

- Stevia (liquid) - GI: 0
- Erythritol - GI: 0
- Aspartame – GI: 0
- Monk Fruit GI: 0
- Inulin – GI: 0
- Xylitol- GI: 13
- Sucralose (liquid) GI: Variable
- Maltitol – GI: 36
- Saccharin – GI: Variable

Choices of Flour

- **Coconut Flour:** Each 1/4 cup of coconut flour contains 19 g of carbohydrates, 6 g of protein, 60 calories, 2.5 g of fat, 12 g of fiber, and 7 g of net carbs. It displays that tropical taste. Be sure it's stored in a closed container. Choose a spot where it's dark such as the pantry. The refrigerator and freezer could cause moisture contamination.

- **Almond Flour:** Almond flour is more of an all-purpose flour and only contains 3 grams of carbs for 1/4 of a cup. (In comparison, totals are overwhelming for the regular wheat flour at 24 grams. This is why it is not on your diet plan!) Almonds are blanched in boiling water to remove the skins and then ground into a fine flour used for baking low-carb cakes, cookies and pie crusts.

- **Almond Meal**: Almond meal isn't the same as almond flour. If you are running low on almond flour for baked goods like muffins and cookies, then merely throw some almonds in a food processor to make some almond meal. The texture is a little different than flour, but the baking results are the same. Almond meal contains 11.1 carbs, 48.2 fat, and 21.8 protein in 100 grams (about 7/8 of a cup).

- **Pumpkin Seed Meal**: You can process raw or toasted pumpkin seeds to make a thick meal. One cup of seeds has 100 calories, 3 net carbs, 9 grams, of protein, and 12 grams of fat.

Avoid Regular Dairy Milk: You would gain 13 grams of carbs for each cup. Choose dairy products that have been cultured and are keto-friendly. The #1 choice is unsweetened almond milk. You can also choose from flax or hemp milk.

Benefits of Pumpkin: Include pumpkin in your 'must have' list. It's full of essential minerals and vitamins including B1, B6, and PP. Carotenes are also in abundance with vitamin A. It has been noted that pumpkin is about 4.5 times higher in vitamin A than carrots. You will notice some of the bread recipes will incorporate pumpkin into its list.

Recognize Healthy Fats

To achieve success in the ketogenic diet, you need fats. These are some of the healthy fats you will want to keep stocked:

Monounsaturated and Saturated Fats: Avocado, butter, coconut oil, egg yolks, and macadamia nuts are some of the recommended categories. These products can be incorporated into your meals using dressings, sauces, or a bit of butter on your meats.

Use non-hydrogenated lards, coconut oil or ghee. Less oxidation occurs in the oil because they have higher smoke points than other oils. Consider these healthy fat options:

- Coconut Oil
- Avocado oil
- Extra-virgin olive oil (EVOO)
- Sesame oil
- Flaxseed oil
- Olives
- Coconut flakes

Nuts & Seeds: Almonds, Walnuts, Pumpkin seeds, chia seeds, flaxseeds, etc.

Use Cinnamon: Use cinnamon as part of your daily plan to improve your insulin receptor activity. As you will see, many of the keto recipes contain the ingredient.

Phases of the Keto Plan

- Standard ketogenic diet (SKD) which consists of high-fat, moderate protein, and is extremely low in carbs.

- Cyclical ketogenic diet (CKD) is created with 5-keto days followed by 2 high-carbohydrate days.

- The high-protein keto (HPK) diet is much like the SKD plan in all aspects other than it has more protein.

- The targeted keto diet (TKD) will provide you with a plan to add carbs to the menu during the times when you are working out.

If you are new to the ketogenic way of eating, you will probably want to use the first method. You can range from 20-50 calories in one day. So, you will want to use your carbs wisely. Each of the recipes in this cookbook is calculated so you will understand how much you can indulge with the delicious muffins, bread, rolls, and other items.

Pitfalls of the Ketogenic Techniques

You have the basics of what the plan is, but now it's time to understand some of the pitfalls of the method. However, each of the issues is an indication that your body is in ketosis. These are a few of the signs you will observe as you begin the transition:

You may experience what is called the 'keto flu' or 'induction flu' which involves lowered mental functions and energy. You may suffer from sleeping issues, bouts of nausea, increased hunger, or other possible digestive worries. Several days into the plan should remedy these effects. If not, add 1/2 of a teaspoon of salt to a glass of water and drink it to help with the side effects. You may need to do this once a day in the first week, and it could take about 15 to 20 minutes before it helps. It will go away!

Leg cramps may be an issue as you begin ketosis. The loss of magnesium (a mineral) can be a demon and create a bit of pain with the onset of the keto diet plan changes. With the loss of the minerals during urination, you could experience bouts of cramps in your legs.

You may also notice an aroma similar to nail polish. Not surprising, because this is acetone, a ketone product. It may also give you a unique body odor as your body adjusts to the diet changes. Maintain good oral health and use a breath refresher if needed. Now, let's see how to prepare these delicious bread items!

Chapter 3: Bread & Biscuits

Bread

Almond Bread

Servings: 4
Macros: 2 g Net Carbs| 8 g Prot. | 24 g Fat | 257 Cal.

What You Need:

- Almond flour – 1 cup
- Whisked eggs - 2
- Baking powder – 1.5 tsp.
- Olive oil – 3 tbsp.
- Also Needed: 3.5 x 8-inch baking pan

How It's Made:

1. Warm up the oven to reach 350°F. Grease the baking pan.
2. Combine all of the components to form a sticky dough.
3. Arrange in the greased tin and bake 30 minutes.
4. Carefully remove the bread and slice into four squares – similar to flatbread.

Cheesy Italian Baked Bread

Servings: 4
Macros: 2.59 g Net Carbs | 16.5 g Prot. | 21.7 g Fat |277 Cal.

What You Need:

- Olive oil – 1 tsp.
- Shredded Monterey jack cheese – 1.25 cups
- Coconut flour – 4 tbsp.
- Italian seasoning – 1 tsp.
- Flaxseed meal – 3 tbsp.
- Egg – 1 Large
- Provolone cheese – 28 grams – 4 slices
- Italian dry salami – 4 small slices
- Fresh spinach leaves – 1 oz.
- Deli sliced mild pepper rings - .25 cup
- Egg yolk – 1 large
- Also Needed: Rolling pin

How It's Made:

1. Warm up the oven to reach 400°F.
2. Combine the seasoning, flaxseed meal, and coconut flour.
3. In another dish, melt the Monterey jack cheese in the microwave until the shreds are fully melted (1 min.). Let it set one minute and add cheese and the whole egg. Mix well. Fold in the dry fixings until it's all mixed.
4. Spread out the dough on a sheet of parchment paper and one on top of the dough. Roll it out where one side is wide enough for the fillings and braid on the other side.

5. Portion the salami and provolone cheese. Next, just tear the spinach to place on top with a layer of the pepper rings, and a spritz of the oil.
6. Use a pizza cutter or sharp knife to slice the sides of the dough into strips (for braiding).
7. Fold-in each end of the bread. Braid the sliced strips on each side.
8. Whisk one of the egg yolks to brush across the top. Put the prepared bread in the oven and bake for 15-20 minutes. Enjoy!

Cloud Bread

Servings: 8
Macros: -0- g Net Carbs| 7 g Prot. | 10 g Fat | 122 Cal.

What You Need:

- Eggs – 3
- Room temperature cream cheese – 3 tbsp.
- Baking powder - .5 tsp.
- Salt – to taste

How It's Made:

1. Separate the egg yolks and whip with the salt and cream cheese.
2. In another dish, whip the baking powder with the egg yolks. Stir together.
3. Warm up the oven to reach 300°F. Line a baking pan with a sheet of the parchment paper.
4. Scoop the dough into the prepared pan – leaving spaces between each one. Bake for 15-20 minutes and enjoy the clouds!

Coconut Bread

Servings: 8
Macros: 3.8 g Net Carbs|9.23 g Prot. | 8.5 g Fat | 154 Cal.

What You Need:

- Baking soda - .5 tsp
- Flaxseed meal - .5 cup
- Sifted coconut flour – 1 cup
- Salt – 1 tsp.
- Baking powder – 1 tsp.
- Room temperature - Large eggs - 6
- Water - .5 cup
- Apple cider vinegar – 1 tbsp.

How It's Made:

1. Warm up the oven in advance to 350F. Lightly grease the baking pan of choice.
2. Sift the flour into a bowl and add the remainder of dry fixings. Mix well.
3. Pour in the vinegar and water to form a thick batter. Press into the prepared pan/pans and bake until browned or for about 40 minutes.
4. Cool in the pan until slightly warm and remove. Slice and serve.

Cottage Bread

Servings: 6
Macros: 6 g Net Carbs |8.4 g Prot. | 6.3 g Fat |109 Cal.

What You Need:

- Ground sesame seeds – 1 tsp.
- Ground flaxseed – 1 tsp.
- Egg – 1
- Cottage cheese - 7-8 oz.
- Turmeric powder - .125 or to taste
- Salt – 1 pinch
- Baking powder - .5 tsp
- Sunflower seeds – 1.5-2 oz.
- Wheat bran – 2 tbsp.
- Oat bran – 3 tbsp.

How It's Made:

1. Combine the sesame seeds, flaxseed, egg, and cottage cheese. Shake in the salt and turmeric. Fold in the seeds and brans. Stir well and let the mixture rest for 10 minutes.
2. Warm up the oven to reach 425°F. Add a sheet of parchment paper to the baking dish.
3. Wet your hands with water and shape the mixture into a ball. Bake for 45 minutes in the preheated oven.

Flax Bread

Servings: 12
Macros: 0.7 g Net Carbs |6 g Prot. | 7.5 g Fat |185 Cal.

What You Need:

- Baking powder – 1 tbsp.
- Flaxseed meal – 2 cups
- Salt – 1 tsp
- Olive oil - .33 cup
- Water - .5 cup
- Whisked eggs – 5
- Maple syrup – 1-2 tbsp.
- Also Needed: 10 x 15-inch pan with sides

How It's Made:

1. Warm up the oven to 350°F. Lightly oil a sheet of parchment paper or use a silicone mat.
2. Whisk all of the dry components and mix with the rest of the wet ingredients. After formed, let it rest for 2-3 minutes to thicken.
3. Pour into the prepared pan – pulling it away from the center for more even baking results. Stretch it into a rectangular shape, leaving about 2 inches from the end of the pan.
4. Bake until it has visible browned and springs back to the touch (24-28 min.).
5. Cool and slice as needed.

Flaxseed Bread with Coconut Flour

Servings: 8

Macros: 3.2 g Net Carbs | 14 g Fat|-not valued-Protein |183 Cal.

What You Need:

- Coconut flour - .75 cup
- Ground flaxseed or flax meal - .5 cup
- Large eggs - 3
- Large egg whites - 3
- Olive oil – 5 tbsp.
- Baking powder – 2 tsp.
- Water - 10 tbsp.
- Sea salt – 1 pinch

How It's Made:

1. Warm up the oven to 350°F. Spritz a baking pan with cooking oil, greasing well.
2. Combine the egg whites and eggs with a processor or electric mixer until foamy. Add the rest of the fixings until the dough is smooth.
3. Let the dough rest for 4-5 minutes so the flax and coconut flours can absorb the moisture.
4. Add to the prepared pan and bake until the top is browned (approximately 35 minutes). If you bake the bread as a loaf, you need to increase the cooking time by 10 minutes. (Muffins – 25-30 min.)
5. Cooking Tip: This loaf is excellent when prepared using a silicone loaf mold.

Garlic Bread with Cheese – Slow-Cooked

Servings: 8
Macros: 5.6 g Net Carbs | 15.29 g Prot. |14.95 g Fat | 224 Cal.

What You Need:

- Cauliflower florets – 12 oz. – 1 medium head
- Italian cheese blend - shredded mozzarella – 2 cups - divided
- Large eggs - 2
- Coconut flour - 3 tbsp.
- Freshly chopped basil - .25 cup
- Pepper - .5 tsp.
- Salt - .5 tsp.
- Minced garlic cloves - 2
- Suggested Size of Cooker: 6-quarts
- Also Needed: Olive oil cooking spray

How It's Made:

1. Grease the sides and bottom of the cooker with the cooking spray. Process the cauliflower until it's rice-like in a food processor.
2. Combine the cheese, eggs, flour, pepper, and salt. Mix well and press firmly into the slow cooker. Sprinkle with the rest of the cheese and garlic.
3. Prepare using the high setting on the slow cooker for 2-4 hours. The cheese will be melted, and edges browned when it is done.
4. Slice and sprinkle with the basil. Enjoy while warm.

Garlic & Cheese Monkey Bread

Servings: 3
Macros: 5.7 g Net Carbs| 8 g Prot. |14.2 g Fat |194 Cal.

What You Need:

- Mozzarella cheese – shredded - .75 cup
- Baby eggplants - 2
- Garlic powder – 1 tsp.
- Dried basil - .25 tsp.
- Melted butter – 2 tbsp.
- Fresh basil – 1 tbsp.
- Also Needed: 3 mini bundt pans

How It's Made:

1. Warm up the oven to 375°F.
2. Remove the ends from the eggplants and cut into cubes. Chop the basil.
3. Combine the dried basil and garlic powder. Mix in with the melted butter.
4. Layer 7-10 cubes of eggplant in each of the mini pans. Sprinkle with some cheese and drizzle with approximately one teaspoon of the garlic mixture.
5. Add another layer of eggplant, cheese, and the remainder of the butter. Garnish with the rest of the cheese.
6. Bake until browned or about 20 minutes. Wait about five minutes before serving. Serve with some low-carb marinara sauce.

Gluten-Free Bread

Servings: 8 slices
Macros: 3 g Net Carbs| 9 g Prot. | 24 g Fat | 267 Cal.

What You Need:

- Salt - .25 tsp.
- Coconut flour – 2 tbsp.
- Baking soda – 1.5 tsp.
- Flaxseed meal - .25 cup
- Almond flour – 1.5 cups
- Eggs – 5
- Coconut oil - .25 cup
- Honey or substitute – 1 tsp.
- Apple cider vinegar – 1 tbsp.

How It's Made:

1. Set the oven temperature to 350°F. Lightly spritz a loaf pan with cooking oil spray.
2. Mix the flaxseed, salt, baking soda, almond flour, and coconut flour in a food processor. Pulse and add the vinegar, oil, and eggs. Pulse and add to the prepared pan.
3. Bake for 1/2 of an hour. Transfer to the counter to cool for about 10 minutes in the pan.
4. Place on a wire rack and finish cooling before storing.

Keto Bread Loaves

Servings: 8
Macros: 2.95 g Net Carbs| 8.2 g Prot. | 8.3 g Fat | 134.3 Cal.

What You Need:

- Large eggs, at room temperature - 6
- Coconut flour - sifted – 1 cup
- Flaxseed meal - .5 cup
- Baking soda - .5 tsp.
- Salt – 1 tsp.
- Baking powder – 1 tsp.
- Water - .5 cup
- Apple cider vinegar – 1 tbsp.

How It's Made:

1. Warm up the oven to reach 350°F. Grease the pans (2 loaf pans), and sift the coconut flour into a container. Combine with the remainder of the dry components and whisk.
2. Stir in the vinegar, water, and eggs. Once it's thick, add the batter to the prepared pans.
3. Bake for 40 minutes and cool in the pan until warm. Remove from the pans and serve.

Low-Carb Cream Cheese Bread

Servings: 6 rolls
Macros: 3 g Net Carbs | 6 g Prot. |21 g Fat | 234 Cal.

What You Need:

- Baking powder – 1 tsp.
- Almond flour – blanched – 1.25 cups
- Psyllium husk powder – 2-5 tbsp.
- Celtic sea salt – 1 tsp.
- Butter – 3 tbsp
- Boiling water – 1 cup
- Large egg – 1
- Cream cheese – 4 oz.

How It's Made:

1. Warm up the oven to reach 350°F.
2. Combine the dry components (baking powder, flour, salt, and psyllium). Set aside.
3. In another glass dish, soften the cream cheese and butter in the microwave or in a saucepan on the stove. Once it's glossy, remove from the burner/microwave and let it cool 2 minutes. Add the eggs and whisk until creamy. Stir in the rest of the components to make the dough.
4. Break into small pieces and add the boiling water to firm up the dough.
5. Use a measuring cup (1/4 cup size) to scoop out the dough. Place on a parchment-lined baking tin to make six rolls of bread.
6. Bake for 45 to 55 minutes and let it cool.

7. Slice the cooled bread using a serrated knife. Serve as it is or with a sandwich.

8. Why not make an extra batch to freeze for emergencies?

Macadamia Bread

Servings: 16
Macros: 5 g Net Carbs | 5 g Prot. |22 g Fat | 227 Cal.

What You Need:

- Macadamia nuts – 2 cups
- Eggs - 4
- Almond flour - .25 cup
- Ground flax seed – 2 tbsp.
- Softened ghee - .25 cup
- Softened coconut butter - .5 cup
- Sea salt – 1 tsp.
- Baking powder - .5 tsp.
- Apple cider vinegar - 2 tbsp.
- Also Needed: 8 x 4 loaf pan

How It's Made:

1. Warm up the oven to 350°F. Lightly grease the pan with ghee.
2. Process the nuts using the S-blade in the food processor until they are a fine flour. Add the eggs - 1 at a time – with the motor running until the mixture is creamy.
3. Fold in the flaxseed, almond flour, coconut butter, ghee, vinegar, sea salt, and baking powder. Continue processing until well combined and pour into the prepared pan.
4. Bake for 35 to 40 minutes.
5. Cool the bread before slicing to serve or store.

Microwave Bread

Serving Size: 4 small rounds
Macros: 2 g Net Carbs| 3.25 g Prot. | 13 g Fat |132 Cal.

What You Need:

- Almond flour - .33 cup
- Salt - .125 tsp
- Baking powder - .5 tsp
- Melted ghee – 2.5 tbsp.
- Whisked egg – 1
- Oil – spritz for the mug

How It's Made:

1. Grease a cup with the oil. Combine all of the fixings in a mixing dish and pour into the cup. Put the cup in the microwave. Set the timer using the high setting for 90 seconds.
2. Transfer the mug to a cooling space for 2-3 minutes. Gently remove from the bread and slice into 4 portions.

Paleo Bread – Keto Style

Servings: 1 loaf – 10 slices
Macros: 9.1 g Net Carbs | 10.4 g Prot. | 58.7 g Fat | 579.6 Cal.

What You Need:

- Olive oil - .5 cup (+) 2 tbsp.
- Eggs – 3
- Almond milk/water - .25 cup
- Coconut flour - .5 cup
- Baking soda – 1 tsp.
- Almond flour – 3 cups
- Baking powder – 2 tsp.
- Salt - .25 tsp.
- Also Needed: Loaf pan – 9 x 5-inches

How It's Made:

1. Warm up the oven to 300°F. Lightly spritz the pan with olive oil.
2. Combine all of the dry fixings and mix with the wet to prepare the dough.
3. Pour into the greased pan and bake for 1 hour.
4. Cool and slice.

Sesame Seed Bread

Servings: 6
Macros: 1 g Net Carbs |7 g Prot. | 13 g Fat | 100 Cal.

What You Need:

- Sesame seeds – 2 tbsp.
- Psyllium husk powder – 5 tbsp.
- Sea salt - .25 tsp.
- Apple cider vinegar – 2 tsp.
- Baking powder – 2 tsp.
- Almond flour – 1.25 cups
- Boiling water – 1 cup
- Egg whites – 3

How It's Made:

1. Heat up the oven to reach 350°F. Spritz a baking tin with some cooking oil spray. Put the water in a saucepan to boil.
2. Combine the almond flour, baking powder, sea salt, sesame seeds, and psyllium powder.
3. Stir in the boiled water, vinegar, and egg whites. Use a hand mixer (less than 1 min.) to combine. Place the bread on the prepared pan.
4. Bake for 1 hour on the lowest rack. Serve and enjoy any time.

Spring Onion Bread

Servings: 6
Macros: 0.5 g Net Carbs| 2.2 g Prot. |1.8 g Fat | 27 Cal.

What You Need:

- Room temperature cream cheese – 3 tbsp.
- Separated eggs – 3
- Apple cider vinegar – 1 tbsp.
- Minced spring onions – 3 tbsp.
- Salt – to taste

How It's Made:

1. Warm up the oven to 300°F.
2. Whisk the egg yolks and combine with the spring onions and cream cheese.
3. In another container, whisk the salt, vinegar, and egg whites.
4. Prepare in batches, starting by adding the egg whites into the egg yolk mixture. Spoon the dough onto a parchment paper-lined pan. Be sure to leave room between each one. Bake for 20 minutes.

Stuffed Savory Bread

Servings:
Macros: 2 g Net Carbs | 6 g Prot. | 20 g Fat | 202 Cal.

What You Need:

- Baking powder – 1.5 tsp.
- Parsley seasoning – 2 tbsp.
- Sage – 1 tsp
- Rosemary – 1 tsp.
- Medium eggs – 8
- Cream cheese – 1 cup
- Butter - .5 cup
- Almond flour – 2.5 cups
- Coconut flour - .25 cup

How It's Made:

1. Heat up the oven to 350F. Grease a loaf pan.
2. Cream/smash the butter and cream cheese. Fold in the seasonings (parsley, sage, and rosemary).
3. Whisk and break in the egg to form the batter until it's smooth.
4. Combine the almond and coconut flour with the baking powder, and add to the mixture until thick.
5. Scoop into the loaf pan and bake for 50 minutes. Serve and enjoy.

Sweet Bread

Banana Bread

Servings: 16
Macros: 8 g Net Carbs | 4 g Prot. | 15 g Fat |165 Cal.

What You Need:

- Baking powder – 1 tsp.
- Stevia 0 .25 tsp.
- Xanthan gum - .5 tsp.
- Salt - .5 tsp.
- Almond flour - .75 cup
- Coconut flour - .33 cup
- Vanilla extract – 1 tsp.
- Medium eggs – 6
- Erythritol - .5 cup
- Coconut oil – 3 tbsp.
- Medium banana – 1
- Melted butter - .5 cup

How It's Made:

1. Warm up the oven to reach 325°F. Grease a loaf pan.
2. Combine the almond and coconut flour with the xanthan gum, stevia, salt, erythritol, and baking powder.
3. Slice the banana and add to a food processor with the butter, oil, eggs, and vanilla extract. Pulse 1 minute and combine with the rest of the fixings. Pulse 1 additional minute until well blended. Pour into the prepared pan and bake for 1 hour and 15 minutes. Serve when the urge strikes.

Cinnabons

Servings: 3
Macros: 1.6 g Net Carbs | 7.4 g Prot.| 7.1 g Fat | 106 Cal.

What You Need:

- Cottage cheese – 6-7 oz.
- Eggs – 2
- Baking powder - .33 tsp.
- Stevia - .25 tsp.
- Coconut flour - .5 cup

What You Need for the Filling:

- Cinnamon – 2 tsp.
- Erythritol – 1 oz.
- Stevia - .25 tsp.
- Melted butter – 2 tbsp.

How It's Made:

1. Warm up the oven to 350°F. Prepare a baking tin with a layer of paper.
2. Mix the cottage cheese, eggs, erythritol, and stevia.
3. Next, fold in the coconut flour and baking powder. Pulse using a blender to mix. You can add additional flour if needed – depending on the moisture content.
4. Arrange the mixture on a layer of plastic wrap; one on the top, and on the counter. Roll out and prepare the dough to a 1/4-inch thickness.
5. Melt the butter. Use a brush to cover the bread. Sprinkle with a dusting of cinnamon. Roll it up and slice it into 8 portions. Arrange on the parchment paper-lined tin and bake for about 15 minutes.

Coconut Balls

Servings: 12
Macros: 6 g Net Carbs | 20.3 g Prot. | 55 g Fat | 144 Cal.

What You Need:

- Egg whites – 3
- Coconut flour – 1 tbsp.
- Coconut flakes – 2.5 oz.
- Your preference of sweetener - .125 or to taste

How It's Made:

1. Cover a baking sheet with parchment paper. Warm up the oven to 395°F.
2. Whisk the eggs until they are foamy.
3. Sift the flour and mix with the coconut flakes, and add to the eggs. (Prepare with a spoon - not the blender.)
4. Form balls and place on the prepared baking tin. Bake for 15 minutes.

Gingerbread – Slow-Cooked

Servings: 10
Macros: 8.6 g Net Carbs| 9.1 g Prot. |24.8 g Fat | 223 Cal.

What You Need:

- Almond or sunflower seed flour – 2.25 cups
- Coconut flour – 2 tbsp.
- Swerve sweetener - .75 cup
- Ground ginger – 1.5 tbsp.
- Dark cocoa powder – 1 tbsp.
- Ground cinnamon - .5 tbsp.
- Salt -.25 tsp.
- Baking powder – 2 tsp.
- Ground cloves - .5 tsp.
- Melted butter - .5 cup
- Water or almond milk - .66 cup
- Large eggs - 4
- Freshly squeezed lemon juice – 1 tbsp.
- Vanilla extract – 1 tsp.
- Suggested Size Cooker: 6-quarts

How It's Made:

1. Prepare the cooker with some cooking spray/oil.
2. Whisk the all of the flour, salt, cloves, baking powder, ginger, cinnamon, sweetener, and cocoa powder in a mixing bowl
3. Blend in the eggs, melted butter, almond milk/water, vanilla extract, and lemon juice.
4. Empty the batter into the slow cooker and cook until set - approximately
2.5-3 hours.
5. Garnish as desired and enjoy, but count those carbs.

Lemon & Blueberry Bread

Servings: 10
Macros: 5 g Net Carbs| 9 g Prot. |17 g Fat |207 Cal.

What You Need:

- Blueberries – 1 cup
- Lemon zested – 1
- Vanilla extract - .5 tsp
- Lemon extract – 1 tbsp.
- Dairy-free mayonnaise – 3 tbsp.
- Medium egg whites – 2
- Whole large eggs – 6
- Salt - .25 tsp.
- Baking soda - .5 tsp.
- Almond flour – 2 cups
- Cream of tartar – 1 tsp.
- Coconut flour - .25 cups
- Stevia - .75 cups

How It's Made:

1. Warm up the oven to reach 350°F. Prepare the bread pan with a layer of parchment paper.
2. Whisk the coconut flour, almond flour, stevia, salt, and baking soda. Fold in the egg whites, whole eggs, mayonnaise, lemon and vanilla extracts, and lemon zest. Combine well with an electric mixer.
3. Stir in half of the berries (.5 cup) and add to the prepared pan. Bake for 20 minutes.

4. Top it off with the remainder of the berries when it is through the first baking. Continue baking for an additional 50 minutes.

5. Allow two hours for the cake to cool. Serve any time.

Pumpkin Bread

Servings: 8
Macros: 5 g Net Carbs | 8 g Prot. | 26 g Fat | 311 Cal.

What You Need:

- Almond flour – 1 cup
- Libby's Canned Pumpkin – 1 small can
- Coconut flour - .5 cup
- Heavy cream - .5 cup
- Stevia - .5 cup
- Melted butter – 1 stick
- Large eggs - 4
- Vanilla – 1.5 tsp.
- Baking powder - .5 tsp.
- Pumpkin spice – 2 tsp.

How It's Made:

1. Program the oven temperature setting at 350ºF. Grease the pan with some coconut oil.
2. Combine all of the fixings in a mixing container until light and fluffy.
3. Empty the batter into the pan. Set a timer for 70 to 90 minutes.
4. Transfer to the counter to cool before serving.

Seedy Pumpkin Bread

Servings:
Macros: 12 g Net Carbs | g Prot. | 16 g Fat | 212 Cal.

What You Need:

- Pumpkin seeds - .25 cup
- Sesame seeds - .25 cup
- Sunflower seeds - .25 cup
- Sugar-free pumpkin puree – canned – 1 cup
- Melted ghee - .25 cup
- Eggs - 4
- Apple cider vinegar – 1 tsp.
- Almond flour – 3 cups
- Baking soda – 1 tsp.
- Coconut flour – .5 cup
- Coconut sugar - .25 cup
- Pumpkin spice – 1 tsp.
- Ground black pepper – 1 pinch
- Sea salt – 1 tsp.
- Chopped rosemary - 2 tbsp.
- Freshly chopped thyme - 1 tbsp.
- Also Needed: Loaf pan

How It's Made:

1. Cover the pan with parchment paper.
2. Preheat the oven to 350°F.
3. Use a cast iron skillet to toast the sunflower seeds, pumpkin seeds, and sesame seeds, frequently stirring until they begin to release an aroma and brown slightly. Transfer to a flat surface and place to the side for now.

4. In a mixing container, mix the eggs, pumpkin, ghee, apple cider vinegar.
5. In another container, combine the dry fixings (coconut flour, almond flour, baking soda, pumpkin spice, pepper, and salt).
6. Add the dry ingredients into the wet and gently mix. Fold in about 3/4 of the seeds, and the rosemary and thyme. Pour the batter into lined pan and top with the remaining seeds.
7. Bake for 45 to 55 minute - checking the center at 45 minutes with a knife or toothpick.
8. Let it cool completely. Then, slice it into 12 portions. Serve warm with ghee or any other way you prefer.

Walnut Bread

Servings: 10

Macros: 11 g Net Carbs| 8 g Prot. | 22 g Fat | 269 Cal.

What You Need:

- Olive oil - .25 cup
- Coconut oil – as needed for the pan
- Medium bananas – 3
- Eggs – 3 Large
- Walnuts - .5 cup
- Almond flour – 2 cups
- Baking soda – 1 tsp.
- Also Needed: A loaf pan

How It's Made:

1. Warm up the oven in advance to 350°F. Lightly grease the pan with the coconut oil.
2. Slice the bananas into circles, and add to a mixing bowl with the rest of the fixings. Use the blender (high setting) to prepare the batter.
3. Pour the batter into the prepared pan. Bake for 50 minutes to 1 hour. Serve warm.

Zucchini Bread – Slow-Cooked

Servings: 12
Macros: 13.8 g Net Carbs | 5 g Prot. | 15.7 g Fat | 174 Cal.

What You Need:

- Cinnamon - 2 tsp.
- Almond flour – 1 cup
- Coconut flour - .33 cup
- Optional: Xanthan gum - .5 tsp.
- Salt - .5 tsp.
- Baking soda - .5 tsp.
- Baking powder – 1.5 tsp.
- Softened coconut oil/butter - .33 cup
- Eggs - 3
- Vanilla – 2 tsp.
- Sweetener – 1 cup or Pyure all-purpose - .5 cup
- Shredded zucchini – 2 cups
- Chopped pecans/walnuts - .5 cup
- Also Needed: 8 x 4 silicone bread pan

How It's Made:

1. Combine the coconut and almond flour, salt, baking soda and powder, xanthan gum, and cinnamon. Set aside for now.
2. Mix the oil, eggs, vanilla, and sugar in another dish. Combine the fixings.
3. Blend in the nuts and shredded zucchini. Scoop the mixture into the prepared bread pan.
4. Arrange the cooker on the top rack (or on crunched up aluminum foil balls). You want it at least 1/2-inch from

the bottom of the slow cooker.

5. Secure the top tightly, and cook for three hours on the high setting.

6. Cool and wrap the bread in a sheet of foil. It's best when refrigerated.

Biscuits

Biscuits & Gravy

Servings: 8
Macros: 5 g Net Carbs| 17.4 g Prot. | 40 g Fat | 460 Cal.

What You Need for the Biscuits:

- Baking powder – 1 tsp.
- Almond flour – 1 cup
- Celtic sea salt - .25 tsp.
- Egg white - 4
- Organic butter/cold coconut oil – 2 tbsp.
- Optional: Garlic or another preferred spice – 1 tsp.

What You Need for the Gravy:

- Chicken/beef broth – 1 cup
- Cream cheese – 1 cup
- Ground black pepper – 1 pinch
- Celtic sea salt – to your liking
- Organic crumbled pork sausage - 1 pkg. (10 oz.)
- Also Needed: Coconut oil cooking spray

How It's Made:

1. Program the oven setting to 400°F. Prepare a muffin pan/cookie sheet with the cooking spray.
2. Cut the butter up into pieces – making sure they are cold. Whisk the whites until fluffy.

3. In another container, combine the flour and baking powder. Cut in the butter and add the salt. Fold in the mixture over the egg whites.
4. Drop the dough onto the baking pan/muffin tin. Bake 11-15 minutes.

Buttery Garlic & Sharp Cheddar Biscuits

Servings: 8
Macros: 0.5 g Net Carbs| 6.7 g Prot. | 12.8 g Fat | 144 Cal.

What You Need:

- Eggs - 4
- Melted – slightly cooled – butter - .25 cup
- Baking powder - .25 tsp.
- Sifted coconut flour - .33 cup
- Salt - .25 tsp.
- Garlic powder - .25 tsp.
- Shredded sharp cheddar cheese - 1 cup

How It's Made:

1. Set the oven temperature to 400°F. Cover a baking tin with a sheet of aluminum foil. Grease with a spritz of oil.
2. Whisk the garlic powder, butter, eggs, and salt together. Fold in the baking powder and flour. Whisk until the lumps are removed. Stir in the cheese, mixing well.
3. Drop by the ice cream scoopful onto the baking pan. Bake about 15 min. Leave it in the pan to cool for 5 to 10 minutes. Remove and serve.
4. They will lose the crispy texture if you don't cool first before you add them to a storage container.

Cheddar Bay Biscuits

Servings: 4 - 8 biscuits – 2 per serving
Macros: 2 g Net Carbs |20 g Fat| 13 g Protein | 230 Cal.

What You Need:

- Shredded mozzarella cheese – 1.5 cups
- Shredded cheddar cheese – 1 cup
- Cream cheese – .5 of 1 pkg. - 4 oz.
- Large eggs – 2
- Almond flour - .66 cup
- Granulated garlic powder - .5 tsp.
- Baking powder - 4 tsp.
- Butter – for the pan

How It's Made:

1. Microwave the cream cheese and mozzarella for about 45 seconds using the high-power setting until melted. Stir and return for 20 additional seconds. Stir once more.
2. In another container, combine the eggs with the almond flour, garlic powder, and baking powder. Mix it all together and place on a sheet of flour-dusted plastic wrap. Roll it up into a ball and place in the fridge for 20-30 minutes.
3. Heat up the oven to reach 425°F. Prepare a dark color baking dish with butter. Slice the cold dough into eight segments. Place in the prepared pan – leaving a little space between each one.
4. Bake for 10-12 minutes. Remove and place on the countertop to cool.

Lavender Biscuits

Servings: 6
Macros: 4 g Net Carbs| 10 g Prot. | 25 g Fat | 270 Cal.

What You Need:

- Coconut oil - .33 cup
- Baking powder – 1 tsp.
- Almond flour – 1.5 cups
- Kosher salt – 1 pinch
- Egg whites - 4
- Culinary grade lavender buds – 1 tbsp.
- Liquid stevia – 4 drops

How It's Made:

1. Warm up the oven until it reaches 350°F. Spritz a baking sheet with a little coconut oil. Mix the coconut oil and almond flour in a container until it's in pea-sized pieces. (It's easier to use your hands.) Set the bowl aside in the fridge.
2. Whisk the eggs until they start foaming. Toss in the salt, lavender, and baking powder. Stir well and mix in the eggs. Add to the almond mixture, stirring well.
3. Place the chunks onto the baking sheet using an ice cream scoop or tablespoon. Pat them, so they aren't round similar to a pancake.
4. Bake for 20 minutes and enjoy.

Cornbread

Jalapeno Cornbread Mini-Loaves

Servings: 8
Macros: 2.96 g Net Carbs| 11.2 g Prot. | 26.8 g Fat | 302 Cal.

What You Need for the Dry Ingredients:

- Almond flour – 1.5 cups
- Golden flaxseed meal - .5 cup
- Salt – 1 tsp.
- Baking powder – 2 tsp.

What You Need for the Wet Ingredients:

- Full fat sour cream - .5 cup
- Melted butter – 4 tbsp.
- Large eggs - 4
- Liquid stevia – 10 drops
- Amoretti sweet corn extract – 1 tsp.

What You Need for the Add-Ins:

- Grated sharp cheddar cheese - .5 cup
- Fresh jalapenos, seeded and membranes removed - 2

How It's Made:

1. Warm up the oven to reach 375°F.
2. Spritz each of the loaf pans with oil cooking spray or butter.

3. Whisk or sift the dry fixings (salt, baking powder, almond flour, and flaxseed meal).

4. In another container, whisk the wet fixings and combine. Fold in the grated cheese and peppers. Pour into the pans and top off each one with a pepper ring.

5. Bake until golden brown or about 20-22 minutes. Leave it in the pan for about five minutes to cool. Then, just place on a wire rack before storing or serving.

Chapter 4: Breadsticks

Breadstick Base – Served 3 Ways

Servings: 6 – 4 breadsticks each

What You Need for the Bread Stick Base

- Mozzarella cheese - 8 oz. – 2 cups
- Almond flour - .75 cup
- Psyllium husk powder – 1 tbsp.
- Cream cheese - 1.5 oz. – 3 tbsp.
- Large egg - 1
- Baking powder – 1 tsp.

Option 1: Cinnamon Sugar

Macros: 3.3 g Net Carbs | 13 g Prot. | 24.3 g Fat | 292 Cal.

What You Need for the Cinnamon Sugar

- Butter – 3 tbsp.
- Swerve sweetener – 6 tbsp.
- Cinnamon – 2 tbsp.

Option 2: Extra Cheesy Breadsticks

Macros: 3.6 g Net Carbs | 25 g Fat|18 g Protein | 314 Cal.

What You Need for the Extra Cheesy

- Garlic powder – 1 tsp.
- Onion powder – 1 tsp.
- Cheddar cheese – 3 oz.
- Parmesan cheese - .25 cup

Option 3: Italian Style Breadsticks

Macros: 2.6 g Net Carbs | 12.8 g Prot. |18.8 g Fat | 238 Cal.

What You Need for the Italian Style:

- Italian seasoning – 2 tbsp.
- Salt & Pepper – 1 tsp. ea.

How It's Made:

1. For any of the types of breadsticks; just warm up the oven to 400°F.
2. Combine the cream cheese and egg until just mixed.
3. In another container, mix each of the dry fixings.
4. Portion the cheese into a microwavable dish and cook at 20-second intervals until sizzling hot. Stir in the cream cheese, eggs, and dry fixings.
5. Knead the dough and press flat using a silpat. Transfer to a piece of foil and slice into pizza forms you like.
6. Bake the pieces for 13-15 minutes on the top rack until crispy. Serve warm.

Flax & Coconut Breadsticks

Servings: 5 – 20 sticks
Macros: 4.2 g Net Carbs |13 g Prot. |27 g Fat | 334 Cal.

What You Need:

- Flax meal/ground flax seed - .75 cup
- Almond flour – 1 cup
- Coconut flour - .25 cup
- Salt – 1 tsp.
- Chia seeds – 2 tbsp.
- Psyllium husk powder – 1 tbsp.
- Lukewarm water – 1 cup (+) 2 tbsp. if the dough is dry

What You Need for the Toppings:

- Mixed seeds - ex. Poppy seed, sesame, or caraway – 4 tbsp.
- Egg yolks – 2 large - For egg-free use water or melted ghee
- Coarse sea salt - pink Himalayan salt – 1 tsp.

What You Need for the Optional Garnishes:

- Marinara sauce
- BBQ sauce
- Keto Cheese sauce
- Pesto

How It's Made:

1. Warm up the oven to reach 350°F.
2. Combine all of the ingredients to form a dough. Work it until it holds together and set it aside for 15-20 minutes.

3. Divide the dough into four segments. Then, into five pieces. Form the stick about ten inches long.
4. Put the breadsticks on a paper-lined baking tin, and brush with the yolks or ghee.
5. Give them a sprinkle of salt, seeds, and parmesan cheese. Be creative and bake for 15-20 minutes until crispy (360°F).

Garlic & Herb Breadstick Bites

Servings: 5 – 9 sticks each
Macros: 2.36 g Net Carbs | 5.4 g Prot. | 4.18 g Fat |135.2 Cal.

What You Need:

- Shredded cheddar cheese - .25 cup
- Cream cheese - softened – 2 oz.
- Almond flour - .5 cup
- Minced garlic – 1 tsp.
- Dried chives – 1 tsp.
- Coconut flour – 1 tbsp.
- Slightly beaten egg white - 1

How It's Made:

1. Warm up the oven to reach 350°F. Prepare a baking tin with a layer of parchment paper.
2. Combine the cheddar and cream cheese in a mixing bowl. Stir in the minced garlic, chives, almond and coconut flour, and egg white. It should not be crumbly or dry, but soft.
3. Add the mixture to a plastic bag. Snip away about a 1-inch corner, or use a pastry bag to pipe the dough onto the baking pan. Make 3-inch strips with the prepared dough. Flatten each one with the tongs of a fork.
4. Bake for 10-15 minutes. Serve hot or chill for a crispier stick.

Oat Sticks

Servings: 10 - 3.5 oz. each
Macros: 7.5 g Net Carbs|4 g Prot. |10.2 g Fat | 137 Cal.

What You Need:

- Finely ground oat flakes – 1 cup
- Almond flour - .5 cup
- Salt – 1 pinch
- Grated cheese – your preference – 2 oz.
- Butter – cubed - 2.5 oz.
- Almond milk – 1 cup

How It's Made:

1. Line a baking tin with parchment paper. Warm up the oven to 375°F.
2. Sift the flour and add the salt and oat flakes.
3. Fold in the cubed butter, grated cheese, and milk.
4. Knead the dough and roll out to a 1/4-inch thickness using a rolling pin. Slice into sticks.
5. Bake until lightly browned or about 12 minutes.

Chapter 5: Pizza Crusts – Flatbread & Pie Crusts

Pizza

Cauliflower Pizza Crust

Servings: 8

Macros: 3 g Net Carbs|10 g Prot. | 6 g Fat | 106 Cal.

What You Need:

- Cauliflower florets – 1.5 cups
- Grated parmesan cheese – 1.5 cups
- Large egg – 1

What You Need for the Optional Fixings:

- Italian seasoning - .5 tbsp.
- Garlic powder - .5 tsp.

How It's Made:

1. Warm up the oven to 400°F. Prepare a pizza pan or stone and line it with a sheet of parchment paper. Pulse the florets using a food processor to make 'riced' cauliflower. On the stovetop, saute the florets about 10 minutes until softened.
2. Whisk the egg and blend in with the cheese and seasonings.

3. Pour the 'rice' into the mixture. Mix well and press with a spatula. It is easier to prepare using two small pizzas.

4. Spread the dough into the pans until about ¼-inch thick. Bake 20 minutes or until browned. Let the crust cool a minimum of 5-10 minutes at room temperature.

5. Add the chosen toppings. Put it in the oven to finish cooking for 5 to 10 more minutes.

Sausage Crust Pizza

Servings: 4
Macros: 12 g Net Carbs | 31.3 g Prot. | 21.2 g Fat | 357 Cal.

What You Need:

- Sausage – 1 lb.
- Diced onion - .5 of 1 small
- Diced red bell pepper – 1
- Sautéed mushrooms – 3 oz.
- Tomato paste – 1 tbsp.
- Mozzarella cheese – 3 oz.
- Sliced ham – 2 oz.
- Onion powder – 1 tsp.
- Garlic powder – 1 tsp.
- Italian seasoning – 1 tsp.
- Also Needed: Medium cake pan

How It's Made:

1. Warm up the oven until it reaches 350°F.
2. Break the sausage apart and smash onto the sides and bottom of the pan.
3. Once loaded, arrange the pan in the heated oven.
4. Bake for 10 to 15 minutes. Transfer it to a platter when done.
5. Combine the garlic powder, tomato paste, Italian seasoning, onion powder, and garlic powder. Sprinkle over the crust.
6. Note: If you choose, you can store the crust in the freezer until ready to prepare if it will be more than a day before you are prepared to use the crust.

7. To prepare, just layer with the ham, onions, mushrooms, and red pepper. Give it a sprinkle of the mozzarella cheese.

8. Cook for 12 to 15 minutes until golden and the cheese is melted.

9. Store in the refrigerator for a couple of days, but no longer. It is best to freeze as soon as it is cooled.

Thin Crust White Pizza

Yields: 4 Servings
Macros: 4.6 g Net Carbs | 20 g Prot. | 28.9 g Fat|352 Cal.

What You Need for the Crust:

- Grated parmesan cheese - .5 cup
- Egg white protein powder – Unflavored - .25 cup
- Pink Himalayan sea salt – .25 tsp.
- Almond flour - .5 cup
- Large egg – 1

What You Need for the Topping:

- Heavy whipping cream – 1 tbsp.
- Cream cheese – 2 tbsp.
- Onion or garlic powder – 1 tsp.
- Hard goat cheese – your favorite – .5 cup
- Feta cheese – Crumbled - .33 cup
- Red onion – 1 small
- Seedless Kalamata olives - .25 cup
- Olive oil – 1 tbsp.

How It's Made:

1. Set the temperature of the oven to 400°F. Line an iron skillet or a cookie sheet with a piece of parchment paper.
2. Whisk each of the dry fixings in a mixing dish. Blend in the egg – mixing by hand. Empty the batter into the baking pan, spreading evenly. Bake for 10-15 min.
3. Prepare the white sauce by mixing the onion/garlic powder, cream cheese, and cream until well combined.

4. Slice the onion. Grate the hard cheese and crumble the feta. You can also chop the olives.
5. Remove the crust when browned and add the white sauce, the cheeses, olives, and onion.
6. Bake 10 minutes or until golden brown. Transfer to the countertop and slice into quarters. Top with some lettuce leaves with a drizzle of the olive oil.

Flatbread

Cheese Flatbread

Servings: 6
Macros: 5 g Net Carbs |12.3 g Prot. | 11.3 g Fat | 170 Cal.

What You Need:

- Warm buttermilk – 1 cup
- Sifted almond flour – 2 cups
- Grated hard cheese – 5.5 oz.
- Baking powder - .5 tsp.
- Salt – a pinch

How It's Made:

1. Warm up the oven to 350°F.
2. Mix the buttermilk with the salt and baking powder.
3. Grate the cheese and combine with the flour. Mix all of the fixings and knead. Make five balls and add them to a parchment paper lined tray.
4. Flatten into five flatbreads and bake 15 minutes. Flip once and cook five more minutes. Serve hot.

Delicious Flatbread

Servings: 6
Macros: 1.8 g Net Carbs | 2 g Prot. |6.6 g Fat |70 Cal.

What You Need:

- Butter – 1 tbsp.
- Salt – 1 pinch
- Sifted almond flour – 8 tbsp.
- Water – 1 cup

How It's Made:

1. Sift the flour and add the salt. Cut in the butter. Pour in the water and knead the dough. Let it rest 15 minutes.
2. Warm up the oven to 350°F.
3. Line the baking sheet with parchment and flatten the dough making several flatbreads.
4. Bake 15 minutes and flip over the bread and bake another 5 minutes.
5. Remove from the pan and enjoy.

Garlic Focaccia

Servings: 8
Macros: 3.4 g Net Carbs| 10.2 g Prot. |19 g Fat | 245 Cal.

What You Need:

- Almond flour – 1 cup
- Baking powder – 1 tsp.
- Ground flaxseed – 1 cup
- Eggs – 6
- Olive oil - .25 cup
- Minced cloves of garlic – 2
- Dried basil – 1 tsp.
- Dried oregano – 1 tsp.
- Salt – 2 pinches

How It's Made:

1. Warm up the oven to reach 350°F.
2. Sift the flour with the spices, baking powder, and flaxseed into a mixing container.
3. One by one add the eggs and garlic, whisking as you go. Add the oil and combine the batter.
4. Line a baking pan with parchment paper and add the batter.
5. Bake for 25 minutes and serve or cool to store.

Ham and Apple Flatbread

Servings: 8
Macros: 5 g Net Carbs|16 g Prot. | 20 g Fat | 255 Cal.

What You Need for the Crust:

- Almond flour - .75 cup
- Grated mozzarella cheese – part-skim – 2 cups
- Cream cheese – 2 tbsp.
- Dried thyme - .125 tsp.
- Sea salt - .5 tsp.

What You Need for the Topping:

- Sliced ham – low-carb – 4 oz.
- Small red onion - .5 of 1
- Grated Mexican cheese – 1 cup
- Apple - .25 of 1 medium
- Dried thyme - .125 tsp.

How It's Made:

1. Discard the core from the apples. You can leave them unpeeled but will need to use a vegetable peeler to make the thin slices.
2. Warm up the oven to 425°F. Cut out 2 sheets of parchment paper to fit into a 12-inch pizza pan. Be sure to cut them about 2 inches larger than the pan.
3. Use the high heat setting. Place a double boiler (water in the bottom pan), and bring the water to boiling, place the heat setting to low.

4. Add the cream cheese, mozzarella cheese, salt, thyme, and almond flour to the top of the double boiler—stirring constantly.

5. When the cheese mixture resembles dough, place it on one of the pieces of parchment—and knead the dough until totally mixed. Roll the dough into a ball—placing it on the center of the paper— put the second piece of paper over the top, and roll with a rolling pin (or a large glass).

6. Place the dough onto the pizza pan (leaving the paper connected).

7. Poke several holes in the dough and put into the preheated oven for approximately six to eight minutes.

8. When browned, remove it and lower the setting of the oven to 350°F.

9. Arrange the cheese, apple slices, onion slices, and ham pieces. Top off with the remainder (.75 cup) of cheese.

10. Flavor with the ground pepper, salt, and thyme.

11. Put into the oven and bake until the cheese melted and the crust is to the desired brown.

12. Slide it from the parchment paper and cool two or three minutes before cutting.

13. Tip: If you do not own a double boiler; you can substitute with a mixing dish over a pot of boiling water as a substitute.

Matzo Bread

Servings: 6
Macros: 1 g Net Carbs | 1 g Prot. |2.2 g Fat | 28 Cal.

What You Need:

- Sifted almond flour – 1 cup
- Water - .5 cup
- Salt – 1 pinch

How It's Made:

1. Warm up the oven ahead of cooking time to 475°F.
2. Sift the flour into a mixing container and add the water one tablespoon at a time. Sprinkle in the salt and knead. Divide into four balls.
3. Paper line a baking tin and add the rolled balls of dough. Flatten into disks and pierce each one to prevent rising.
4. Bake for two minutes per side.

Pita Bread

Servings: 8
Macros: 1.6 g Net Carbs| 1.6 g Prot. | 6.9 g Fat |73 Cal.

What You Need:

- Sifted almond flour – 2 cups
- Water - .5 cup
- Olive oil – 2 tbsp.
- Salt- 1 pinch
- Black cumin – 1 tsp.

How It's Made:

1. Preheat the oven setting to 400°F. Line a baking tin with paper.
2. Whisk the salt with the flour. Work in the water and oil.
3. Knead the dough and let it rest for 15 minutes. Shape the dough into eight balls. Arrange the prepared dough balls on the paper-lined pan and flatten. Sprinkle with the cumin and bake for 15 minutes.

Tart Pie Crust

Servings: 5 Crusts
Macros: 3.3 g Net Carbs| 6.5 g Prot. | 15.3 g Fat | 193 Cal.

What You Need:

- Almond flour - .5 cup
- Coconut flour - .5 cup
- Psyllium husk powder – 2 tbsp.
- Coconut oil – 2 tbsp.
- Large eggs – 2
- Ice cold water – 5 tbsp.
- Salt - .25 tsp.
- Also Needed: 5 tart pans

How It's Made:

1. Combine all of the dry fixings in a bowl. Fold in the oil to form a sandy consistency. Whisk the egg and water into the mixture. Knead and slice into 5 chunks.
2. Work the dough into each of the pie pans and bake for 12-15 minutes (partially cooked). Fill with the desired fixings and cook for 20-30 more minutes or as the recipe requires.

Chapter 6: Muffins

Apple & Almond Muffins

Servings: 12 – if using silicone molds
Macros: 10 g Net Carbs | 5 g Prot.| 15 g Fat | 184 Cal.

What You Need:

- Almond flour – 2.5 cups
- Cinnamon – 1 tsp.
- Eggs – 2
- Melted butter - .33 cup
- Maple syrup – 4 tbsp.
- Thinly sliced apple - 1

How It's Made:

1. Preheat the oven to 350°F.
2. Mix all of the fixings – omitting the apple.
3. Peel and fold the apple slices and pour the dough into the cups.
4. Bake for 15 minutes and cool before storing.

Bacon & Asparagus Muffins

Servings: 12 – 3 each
Macros: 3 g Net Carbs|19 g Prot. | 41 g Fat | 460 Cal.

What You Need:

- Diced bacon slices - 4
- Whisked eggs - 8
- Asparagus spears – 7-8 or 1 cup
- Chopped onions – 2 tbsp.
- Pepper and salt – to your liking
- Coconut milk – canned - .5 cup

How It's Made:

1. Warm up the oven until it reaches 350°F.
2. Cook the bacon in a frying pan. Drain on a towel and dice when cooled.
3. Combine all of the fixings and add to 12 mini quiche cups.
4. Bake until the center stops jiggling or about 25-30 minutes.

Bacon & Cheese Cauliflower Muffins

Servings: 6 – 2 nests
Macros: 2.4 g Net Carbs|6.6 g Prot. | 8 g Fat | 110 Cal.

What You Need:

- Shredded cheddar cheese – 1 cup
- Cauliflower rice – 3 cups
- Baking powder – 1 tsp.
- Almond flour - .25 cup
- Oregano – 1 tbsp.
- Chopped bacon – 7 slices
- Garlic powder – 1 tbsp.
- Parsley – 1 tbsp.
- Salt and pepper - to taste
- Paprika – 1 tbsp.
- Large eggs - 2
- Crumbled feta - .25 cup

How It's Made:

1. Warm up the oven to 350°F.
2. Prepare the riced cauliflower in a hefty container. Fold in each of the dry fixings with the bacon and cheese. Whisk and add the eggs and mix well.
3. Prepare a 12-count muffin tin with baking cups. Add the mixture to each one and top with the feta cheese.
4. Bake for 35 minutes and enjoy!

Brownie Muffins

Servings: 6
Macros: 4.4 g Net Carbs| 7 g Prot. | 13 g Fat | 183 Cal.

What You Need:

- Salt - .5 tsp.
- Flaxseed meal – 1 cup
- Cocoa powder - .25 cup
- Cinnamon – 1 tbsp.
- Baking powder - .5 tbsp.
- Coconut oil – 2 tbsp.
- Large egg- 1
- Sugar-free caramel syrup - .25 cup
- Vanilla extract - 1 tsp.
- Pumpkin puree - .5 cup
- Slivered almonds - .5 cup
- Apple cider vinegar – 1 tsp.

How It's Made:

1. Set the oven temperature to 350°F.
2. Use a deep mixing container — mix all of the fixings and stir well.
3. Use six paper liners in the muffin tin, and add 1/4 cup of batter to each one. Sprinkle several almonds on the tops, pressing gently.
4. Bake approximately 15 minutes or when the top is set.

Cheeseburger Muffins

Servings: 9
Macros: 2.97 g Net Carbs| 14.6 g Prot. | 19.67 g Fat |255.67 Cal.

What You Need for the Muffin Buns:

- Blanched almond flour - .5 cup
- Flaxseed meal - .5 cup
- Baking powder – 1 tsp.
- Salt - .5 tsp
- Pepper - .25 tsp
- Large eggs - 2
- Sour cream - .25 cup

What You Need for the Hamburger Filling:

- Ground beef – 16 oz.
- Onion powder - .5 tsp.
- Garlic powder - .5 tsp.
- Tomato paste – 2 tbsp.
- Salt and pepper - to taste

What You Need for the Toppings:

- Cheddar cheese - .5 cup
- Baby dill pickles - 1 pickle - 18 slices
- Reduced sugar ketchup – 2 tbsp.
- Mustard – 2 tbsp.

How It's Made:

1. Sear the beef in a hot pan with the seasonings.
2. Mix the dry fixings with the wet ones. Warm up the oven to 350°F.
3. Pour into silicone muffin cups. Indent the center to make a space for the beef and fill.
4. Bake for 15-20 minutes. Remove and top with cheese and broil for one to three minutes. Cool for 5 to 10 minutes and remove from the cups. Serve.

Cinnamon & Apple Spiced Muffins

Servings: 12
Macros: 4 g Net Carbs|7 g Prot. | 17 g Fat | 198 Cal

What You Need:

- Super-fine almond flour – 2.5 cups
- Cinnamon - 1 tsp.
- Granulated stevia - erythritol blend – .75 cup
- Sea salt – .5 tsp.
- Baking powder - 1 tsp.
- Melted coconut oil or butter – .25 cup
- Large eggs – 4
- Vanilla extract - 1 tsp.
- Almond milk – Unsweetened - .25 cup
- Granny Smith apple – 1 – 4 oz.

How It's Made:

1. Warm up the oven to 350°F. Add liners to a 12-count muffin tin or spritz with some oil.
2. Whisk the stevia, salt, cinnamon, baking powder, and flour in a mixing container. Fold in the coconut oil or butter to make a crumbly mixture.
3. Mix the milk, extract, and eggs in another container. Combine the fixings. Peel, slice and finely dice the apple and add to the batter.
4. Fill each of the cups about 3/4 of the way to the top.
5. Bake until it springs back when gently touched (approx. 25-30 min.).
6. Leave the muffins in the baking tin for 5-10 minutes. Arrange the muffins on a wire rack to finish cooling.
7. Enjoy when cooled or set aside for when you want a delicious snack.

Cinnamon & Applesauce Muffins

Servings: 12
Macros: 3 g Net Carbs|7 g Prot. | 22 g Fat | 241 Cal.

What You Need:

- Melted ghee - .5 cup
- Large whisked eggs - 3
- Nutmeg – 1 tsp.
- Cinnamon – 3 tbsp.
- Almond flour – 3 cups
- Cloves - .25 tsp.
- Applesauce – 4 tbsp.
- Baking powder – 1 tsp.
- Stevia - to taste
- Lemon juice – 1 tsp.
- Muffin tins with paper or silicone cups – 12-count

How It's Made:

- Set the oven temperature to 350°F.
- Combine the ingredients in a mixing container. Empty the batter into the muffin tins. Bake for about 17-20 minutes until the center is springy.
- Cool before storing.

Eggplant Muffins

Servings: 3
Macros: 5.7 g Net Carbs| 8 g Prot. |14.2 g Fat | 194 Cal.

What You Need:

- Garlic powder – 1 tsp.
- Dried basil - .5 tsp.
- Peeled & cubed eggplant - 2
- Mozzarella cheese - .75 cup
- Melted butter – 2 tbsp.
- Chopped fresh basil – 1 tbsp.

How It's Made:

1. Warm up the oven to reach 375°F.
2. Melt the butter and combine with the dried basil and garlic powder.
3. Cube the eggplant and add to 3 baking cups. Sprinkle with the mozzarella cheese and 1 teaspoon of the butter mixture. Add a layer of eggplant, cheese, and butter. Top it off with the rest of the cheese.
4. Bake until golden brown or about 20 minutes.

English Muffins

Servings: 1
Macros: 2.5 g Net Carbs| 8 g Prot. |12 g Fat | 200 Cal.

What You Need:

- Melted butter or coconut oil - .5 tbsp.
- Whisked egg – 1
- Unsweetened almond or coconut milk – 1 tbsp. or Half & Half
- Coconut flour – 1 tbsp.
- Baking powder - .5 tsp.
- Vanilla Extract - .125 tsp. - optional
- Liquid Stevia - optional – 6 drops
- Sea Salt - optional – 1 pinch

How It's Made:

1. Warm up the oven to 400°F. Melt the oil/butter in a ramekin. Add the remainder of the fixings to the bowl. Stir quickly until the clumps are gone.
2. Prepare in the microwave for 1.5 minutes or bake for 12-15 minutes.
3. Loosen the edges and transfer to a cutting surface. Slice in half sideways.
4. Lightly brown on each side in a skillet prepared with oil or butter. This is a vital step, so don't skip it. Gently press the muffins in the pan with the spatula as they toast.

Ham Muffins

Servings: 12
Macros: 1.5 g Net Carbs | 10 g Prot.| 9 g Fat | 129 Cal.

What You Need:

- Ham – 12 oz.
- Green pepper - .25 cup
- Celery – 1 stalk
- Pepper - .25 tsp.
- Onion powder - .25 tsp.
- Freshly chopped parsley – 1 tbsp.
- Minced chives – 1 tbsp.
- Cayenne – 1 dash
- Shredded cheddar cheese – 6 oz.
- Eggs - 3

How It's Made:

1. Line a rimmed baking sheet with a layer of aluminum foil for possible spills. Spritz the muffin tins with some cooking spray or oil.
2. Mince the celery and green pepper. Also, finely mince the ham in a food processor. Mix all of the fixings thoroughly. Spoon into the muffin tins sitting on the cookie sheet.
3. Bake for 30-35 minutes until browned.
4. Cool for 10 minutes on a wire rack. Enjoy piping hot or later as a snack.

Lemon Coconut Muffins

Servings: 16
Macros: 2 g Net Carbs| 3 g Prot. | 7 g Fat | 78 Cal.

What You Need:

- Erythritol - .25 cup
- Butter - .25 cup
- Eggs – 3
- Coconut flour - .25 cup
- Coconut flakes - .5 cup
- Baking powder - .5 tsp.
- Vanilla extract - .5 tsp.
- Coconut milk – 3 tbsp.
- Lemon – juiced & zest - 1

How It's Made:

1. Warm up the oven to 400°F. Lightly grease 16 muffin tins. Whisk the erythritol and butter together until creamy smooth.
2. Break the eggs in one at a time. Add the lemon juice, zest, milk, and vanilla extract. Fold in the baking powder, sifted flour, and flaked coconut.
3. Scoop the dough into the baking pan. Prepare for 20 minutes in the heated oven. Cool slightly and enjoy. Cool thoroughly before storing.

Lemon Poppyseed Muffins

Servings: 12
Macros: 1 g Net Carbs | 4 g Prot.| 13 g Fat | 141 Cal.

What You Need:

- Eggs - 3
- Full-fat ricotta cheese - .25 cup
- Coconut oil - .25 cup
- Poppy seeds – 2 tbsp.
- True lemon packets - 4
- Heavy whipping cream - .25 cup
- Lemon extract – 1 tsp.
- Almond flour – 1 cup
- Swerve or alternative sweetener - .33 cup
- Baking powder – 1 tsp.

How It's Made:

1. Heat up the oven to 350°F. Prepare a 12-count muffin tin with silicone cupcake liners.
2. Combine all of the fixings until smooth. Scrape the mixture into the cups.
3. Bake for 40 minutes. Insert a knife or toothpick in the middle of the muffin to check for doneness. Chill for several minutes before taking them from the liners.

Pesto Egg Muffins

Servings: 10
Macros: 1.2 g Net Carbs | 6.9 g Prot.| 10 g Fat | 125 Cal.

What You Need:

- Pesto – 3 tbsp.
- Frozen spinach - .66 cup
- Pitted Kalamata olives - .5 cup
- Chopped sun-dried tomatoes - .25 cup
- Large eggs - 6
- Feta - soft goat cheese – 4.4 oz.
- Pepper and salt – Ex. Himalayan salt – to taste

Also Needed:

- Muffin Tin
- Bowl cups

How It's Made:

1. Heat up the oven to 350°F.
2. Prep the Veggies: Thaw and remove the excess liquid from the spinach or blanch a portion of freshly picked spinach for one minute in boiling water. Transfer the cooked veggies into an ice bath to stop the cooking process. Chop the tomatoes and slice the olives.
3. Whisk in the pesto, salt, and pepper – mixing well. Divide the fixings evenly into the 10 cups– starting with the spinach, cheese, tomatoes, and olives. Blend in the pesto and egg mixture.
4. Bake until browned for approximately 20-25 minutes.

5. When the muffins are done, set them on a cooling rack for a short time.

6. You can store the tasty breakfast treats in the fridge for five days or so.

Pistachio Muffins

Servings: 12
Macros: 3 g Net Carbs| 6 g Prot. |17 g Fat | 198 Cal.

What You Need:

- Large brown eggs – 4
- Unsalted butter - .5 cup
- Swerve confectioners - .25 cup
- Large brown eggs – 4
- Organic stevia blend – ex. Pyure - .25 cup
- Vanilla extract – 1 tsp.
- Pistachio extract – 1 tsp.
- Almond mild original/Unsweetened/Plain - .5 cup
- Blanched almond flour – 1 cup
- Organic coconut flour – Gluten-Free - .5 cup
- Baking powder – 2 tsp.
- Xanthan gum - .5 tsp.
- Himalayan Pink Salt – 1 tsp.
- Pistachio nuts crushed - .5 cup

How It's Made:

1. Warm up the oven to reach 325°F.
2. In a large mixing bowl, whisk the eggs. In another container, melt the butter until softened. Next, just add the sweeteners, almond milk, and each of the extracts. Mix well.
3. In a medium container, add the rest of the fixings – omitting the pistachios.

4. Whisk, making sure there are no clumps. Add the dry ingredients into a large bowl and mix well. Fold in the crushed pistachios until blended.

5. Grease 12 muffin cups or use liners. Pour the batter evenly into each well.

6. Gently tap the container to release any air bubbles

7. Bake for 25-30 minutes. Let cool before removing.

Pumpkin Muffins

Servings: 5
Macros: 3.5 g Net Carbs| 7.4 g Prot. | 13.5 g Fat | 185 Cal.

What You Need:

- Salt - .5 tsp.
- Baking powder - .5 tsp.
- Egg – 1
- Vanilla extract – 1 tbsp.
- Apple cider vinegar – 1 tbsp.
- Pumpkin puree - .5 cup
- Coconut oil – 2 tbsp.
- Sugar-free caramel syrup - .25 cup
- Optional: Crushed almonds - .25 cup

How It's Made:

1. Warm up the oven to 350°F. Combine all of the components in the recipe list except for the almonds.
2. Prepare a muffin pan for 5 portions. If you are using the almonds, spritz with some of the oil. Bake for 15-18 minutes. Enjoy for breakfast or on-the-go.

Pumpkin Maple Flaxseed Muffins

Servings: 10
Macros: 2 g Net Carbs| 5 g Prot. | 8.5 g Fat | 120 Cal.

What You Need:

- Ground flaxseeds – 1.25 cups
- Baking powder - .5 tbsp.
- Erythritol - .33 cup
- Salt - .5 tsp.
- Cinnamon – 1 tbsp.
- Pumpkin pie spice – 1 tbsp.
- Coconut oil – 2 tbsp.
- Pure pumpkin puree – 1 cup
- Egg - 1
- Maple syrup - .5 cup
- Apple cider vinegar - .5 tsp.
- Vanilla extract - .5 tsp.
- Topping: Pumpkin seeds

Also Needed:

- Blender such as NutriBullet
- Muffin tin – 10 sections with silicone liners

How It's Made:

1. Heat the oven to 350°F. Prepare the muffin tin with cupcake liners.
2. Toss the seeds into the blender about 1 second – no longer or it could become damp.

3. Combine the dry fixings and whisk until well mixed. Add the puree, vanilla extract, and pumpkin spice along with the maple syrup (.5 tsp.) if using. Blend in the oil, egg, and apple cider vinegar. Combine nuts or any other fold-ins of your choice, but also add the carbs.

4. Scoop the mixture out by the tablespoon into the prepared tins. Garnish with some of the pumpkin seeds. Leave a little space in the top since they will rise.

5. Bake approximately 20 minutes. They are ready when they are slightly browned. Let them cool a few minutes and add some ghee or butter or some more syrup.

Squash Muffins

Servings: 6
Macros: 3.4 g Net Carbs| 7.3 g Prot. | 7.8 g Fat | 111 Cal.

What You Need:

- Salt – to taste
- Baking powder - .66 tsp.
- Almond flour – 1 cup
- Peeled & grated squash – 1
- Chopped spring onions – 2-3 sprigs
- Olive oil – 1 tbsp.
- Egg – 1
- Plain yogurt - .25 cup
- Grated hard cheese - .5 cup

How It's Made:

1. Warm up the oven to 350°F. Spritz six muffin tins with cooking oil spray.
2. Season the grated squash with salt and set aside.
3. Combine the baking powder, salt, and sifted flour.
4. Whisk the egg, and mix with the oil, 1/2 of the cheese, and yogurt. Combine the fixings.
5. Add the squash and juices to the dough. Work in the chopped onions and add to the prepared muffin cups (1/2 full). Sprinkle with the cheese and bake for 25 minutes.
6. Cool slightly and serve. Store in the fridge when cooled if you have leftovers.

Chapter 7: Bagels

Bagels with Cheese

Servings: 6
Macros: 8 g Net Carbs |31 g Fat| 19 g Prot. | 374 Cal.

What You Need:

- Baking powder – 1 tsp.
- Almond flour – 1.5 cups
- Shredded mozzarella cheese – 2.5 cups
- Cream cheese – 3 oz.
- Eggs – 2

How It's Made:

1. Set the oven temperature to 400°F.
2. Combine the flour, baking powder, mozzarella, and cream cheese in a mixing bowl. Place in the microwave to melt for about 1 minute. Stir well.
3. Let the mixture cool and add the eggs. Break apart into six sections and shape into round bagels.
4. Note: You can also sprinkle with a seasoning of your choice or pinch of salt if desired. Bake until the edges of the bagels are golden brown (12 to 15 min.).
5. Cool and store.

Everything Bagels

Servings: 6 bagels – 1 each
Macros: 6 g Net Carbs | 27.8 g Prot. | 35.5 g Fat | 449 Cal.

What You Need:

- Almond flour – 2 cups
- Baking powder – 1 tbsp.
- Garlic powder – 1 tsp.
- Onion powder – 1 tsp.
- Dried Italian seasoning – 1 tsp.
- Large eggs – divided – 3
- Shredded low moisture mozzarella cheese – 3 cups
- Cream cheese – 5 tbsp.
- Everything Bagel Seasoning – see recipe below – 3 tbsp.

How It's Made:

1. Warm up the oven to 425°F. Use a silpat/parchment paper to line a rimmed baking sheet.
2. Sift and combine the almond flour, Italian seasoning, onion powder, garlic powder, and baking powder.
3. Crack and whisk one of the eggs to be used for the bagel tops and set aside; the others are for the dough.
4. Prepare a microwave-safe container using the cream cheese and mozzarella cheese. Cook 1.5 minutes. Stir and return for 1 more minute.
5. In another mixing container add the 2 eggs and the almond flour mixture. Combine well and divide into six segments. (Tip: If the dough gets stiff; just add it back in the microwave for 30 seconds to soften.)

6. Roll into balls and press your finger in the center of each one to form the ring. Make a small hole in each one with the egg wash (step 4). Top with the below *Bagel Seasoning* and bake until golden brown (12-14 minutes).

7. If you want to freeze the bagels, be sure to slice them into halves first to make the warm-up process easier.

Bagel Seasoning

Servings: 1 cup
Macros Per 2 Tablespoons: 2.6 g Net Carbs | 0.8 g Prot.| 15 g Fat | 61 Cal.

What You Need:

- Toasted sesame seeds - .25 cup
- Coarse sea salt – 2 tbsp.
- Poppy seeds – Dried minced onions – dried garlic flakes – 3 tbsp (+) 1 tsp. each

How It's Made:

1. Combine all of the fixings and store in a closed container.
2. Always, shake before using.

Cinnamon Raisin Bagels

Servings: 6
Macros: 6.2 g Net Carbs | 3 g Prot. | 10 g Fat | 139 Cal.

What You Need:

- Coconut flour sifted - .33 cup
- Golden flax meal – 1.5 tbsp
- Baking soda - .5 tsp or Baking powder -1 tsp.
- Cinnamon – 2 tsp. – optional – omit if making plain bagels
- Optional: Sea salt – a dash
- Whisked eggs – 3
- Unsweetened coconut or almond milk - .33 cup
- Butter – coconut oil or ghee – melted – 2.5 tbsp.
- Apple cider vinegar – 1 tsp.
- Liquid stevia – 1 tsp.
- Optional: Vanilla extract – 1 tsp.
- Golden raisins - .33 cup

How It's Made:

1. Warm up the oven to 350°F. Grease a donut/bagel pan.
2. Mix the dry fixings (the golden flax meal, the sifted coconut flour baking soda or baking powder, cinnamon, and sea salt thoroughly.
3. In another container, mix the almond/coconut milk, apple cider vinegar, eggs, melted butter/coconut oil, vanilla extract, and stevia.
4. Combine all of the fixings and add to the prepared pan – spreading evenly with a spatula.

5. Bake at 350°F for 17-20 minutes. Set aside to cool for a few minutes. Loosen the bagels with a knife. Turn the bread on the side and slice into half.

6. Serve with a topping of your choice; such as butter or cream cheese.

7. Refrigerate or freeze unused portions.

Croissant Bagels

Servings: 7
Macros: 1.1 g Net Carbs | 3.4 g Prot. | 0.7 g Fat | 83 Cal.

What You Need:

- Eggs – separated – 3
- Softened cream cheese – 2 tbsp.
- Cream of tartar .25 tsp
- Melted butter – 2 tbsp.
- Sifted coconut flour – 2 tbsp.
- Sweetener of choice: Erythritol – 1.5 tsp. or Liquid stevia – 15 drops
- Baking soda - .5 tsp. (+) Cream of tartar - .25 tsp. – mixed together
- Sea salt - .125 tsp.
- Also Needed: Donut/bagel pan

How It's Made:

1. Warm up the oven to 300°F.
2. Lightly spritz the pan with cooking oil spray.
3. Separate the egg whites from the yolks.
4. Add the cream of tartar to the egg whites. Whisk using the chosen mixer until stiff peaks form. Sit to the side for now.
5. Beat the egg yolks in separate mixing bowl and combine with the melted butter, cream cheese, the cream of tartar mixture, baking soda, coconut flour, sweetener of choice, and sea salt. Continue beating until the egg yolk mixture is thoroughly incorporated.

6. Gently fold in (do not whisk) the egg yolk mixture into egg white mixture until combined. Spoon the mixture into the pan.

7. Bake for 20-25 minutes. Once it's done, remove and cool.

Garlic Coconut Flour – Gluten-Free Bagels

Servings: 6 Bagels
Macros: 3 g Net Carbs| 8 g Prot. | 16 g Fat | 191 Cal.

What You Need:

- Melted butter - .33 cup
- Garlic powder – 1.5 tsp
- Sifted coconut flour - .5 cup
- Eggs – 6
- Salt - .5 tsp.
- Baking powder - .5 tsp.
- Optional: Xanthan gum/Guar gum – 2 tsp.
- Also Needed: Donut Pan

How It's Made:

1. Grease the donut pan and warm up the oven to 400°F.
2. Combine the butter, garlic powder, eggs, and salt.
3. In another dish, combine the baking powder, coconut flour, and xanthan gum – if you're using it. Whisk the fixings together until the lumps are removed.
4. Spoon into the donut pan. Bake for 15 minutes. Let them cool in the pan (left in the oven) 10 to 15 minutes. Serve or cool thoroughly before storing.

Mozzarella Bagels

Servings: 6
Macros: 6 g Net Carbs | 12 g Prot. | 21 g Fat | 245 Cal.

What You Need:

- Shredded mozzarella – 1.5 cups
- Cream cheese – diced pieces – 2 oz.
- Oat fiber – 1 tbsp.
- Almond flour – 1.5 cups
- Baking powder – 1 tsp.
- Egg – 1

How It's Made:

1. Put the cream cheese and mozzarella in the microwave for 1 minute. Stir and cook for another 30 seconds.
2. Use a food processor to mix the cheese and egg. Work in the dry fixings.
3. Scrap the dough into plastic wrap and put in the freezer 20 minutes.
4. Warm up the oven to 400°F and prepare a baking tin with a sheet of parchment paper. Take the dough from the freezer and shape into six segments. Roll each one into a sausage-shape and form a bagel ring.
5. Place on the paper to bake for 12-15 minutes

Onion Bagels – Gluten-Free

Servings: 6
Macros: 1 g Net Carbs | 5 g Prot.| 5 g Fat | 78 Cal.

What You Need:

- Coconut flour – 2 tbsp.
- Flaxseed meal – 3 tbsp.
- Baking powder - .5 tsp.
- Separated eggs – 4
- Dried minced onion – 1 tsp.

How It's Made:

1. Warm the oven to reach 325°F. Mist a donut baking pan with a cooking oil spray.
2. Sift the coconut flour, flax meal, minced onion, and baking powder.
3. Whip the egg whites until foamy using an electric mixer. Slowly whisk in the yolks and dry mixture. Let the dough thicken for 5-10 minutes.
4. Scoop into the molds and sprinkle with a portion of dried onion to your liking.
5. Bake until golden brown or about 30 minutes. Cool the bagels in the oven.

Poppy & Sesame Seed Bagels

Servings: 6

Macros: 5 g Net Carbs | 29 g Fat | 20 g Protein | 350 Cal.

What You Need:

- Sesame cheese – 8 tsp.
- Poppy seeds – 8 tsp.
- Shredded mozzarella cheese – 2.5 cups
- Baking powder – 1 tsp
- Almond flour – 1.5 cups
- Large eggs – 2

How It's Made:

1. Set the oven temperature to 400°F. Prepare a baking sheet with a layer of parchment paper. Combine the almond flour and baking powder.
2. Melt the mozzarella and cream cheese in a microwave-safe dish for 1 minute, stir, and cook 1 additional minute (2 minutes total).
3. Whisk the eggs and add the cheese mixture. Stir and combine with the rest of the fixings. Once the dough is formed, break it apart into six pieces.
4. Stretch the dough and join the ends to form the bagel. Arrange on the baking sheet. Sprinkle with the seed combination and bake for 15 minutes.

Pumpkin Bagels

Servings: 8
Macros: 2.6 g Net Carbs | 3 g Prot.| 5 g Fat | 82 Cal.

What You Need:

- Golden flax meal – 3 tbsp.
- Coconut flour sifted - .33 cup
- Whisked eggs – 3
- Melted butter or coconut oil – 2 tbsp.
- Unsweetened almond or coconut milk - .25 cup
- Pure pumpkin puree - .5 cup
- Pumpkin pie spice – 1.25 tsp.
- Vanilla extract – 1 tsp.
- Sea salt - .125
- Cinnamon - .5 tsp.
- Erythritol – 1.5 tbsp. (+) Stevia liquid – 15 drops
- Baking soda - .5 tsp. (+) Apple cider vinegar – 1 tsp.

How It's Made:

1. Warm up the oven to 350°F.
2. Generously spritz a bagel or donut pan with the oil.
3. Sift the coconut flour and combine with the cinnamon, golden flax meal, sea salt, and pumpkin pie spice. Stir and sit to the side for now.
4. In another mixing container, mix the milk, eggs, sweetener, pumpkin puree, vanilla extract, and melted butter/oil.
5. Combine the baking soda and apple cider vinegar together and add to the egg mixture. Incorporate

everything and stir thoroughly until the batter is smooth.

6. Scoop the batter into the pan forms and spread around evenly. Bake until the tops are browned and firm (approx. 25 min.).

7. Once it is done, leave it in the pan to cool. You can serve it whole, or sliced in half. Refrigerate overnight for a firmer bread.

8. Note: It can be pan-toasted on each side in a frying pan with a little butter or coconut oil, and flipped over to brown both sides. You can also use a toaster oven. Don't use a regular – *pop-up* toaster. Serve with a portion of cream cheese or butter.

Chapter 8: Buns & Rolls

Buns

Basil Buns

Servings: 8
Macros: 1.4 g Net Carbs | 9.6 g Prot. | 15 g Fat | 186 Cal.

What You Need:

- Water - .75 cup
- Butter – 6 tbsp.
- Salt – 1 pinch
- Chopped fresh basil – 1 cup
- Crushed garlic cloves – 6
- Eggs – 4
- Almond flour - .75 cup
- Grated Parmesan – 5.5 oz

How It's Made:

1. Warm up the oven to 400°F. Line a baking sheet with a sheet of parchment paper.
2. Boil the water and add the salt and butter. Remove from the heat and add the flour. Combine well, and break in the eggs 1 at a time.
3. Stir in the garlic, basil and lastly the parmesan.
4. Once it's creamy, add the dough on the prepared pan one spoonful at a time shaping into buns.
5. Bake for 20 minutes and enjoy. Cool before storing.

Breakfast Buns

Servings: 4
Macros: 4 g Net Carbs | 9.4 g Prot. | 26 g Fat | 309 Cal.

What You Need:

- Whole flax seeds – 1 tbsp.
- Psyllium husk powder – 2 tbsp.
- Baking powder – 1 tsp.
- Almond flour - .75 cup
- Salt - .5 tsp.
- Olive oil – 2 tbsp.
- Sour cream - .5 cup
- Eggs – 2
- Shelled sunflower seeds – 1 tbsp.

How It's Made:

1. Heat up the oven to reach 400°F. Line a cake pan using a sheet of parchment paper.
2. Mix the dry ingredients (psyllium, flour, baking powder, salt, and seeds).
3. Combine the eggs, sour cream, oil, and eggs. Fold into the dry fixings. Let it rest for 5 minutes (significant).
4. Slice the dough into four portions and shape into a ball. Arrange the balls in the pan and bake for 20-25 minutes.
5. Tip: If the dough mixture is still sticky to touch, just use a few drops of oil on your hands while working with the dough.

Buns for Burgers

Servings: 12

Macros: 3.1 g Net Carbs | 11.6 g Prot. | 12.6 g Fat | 189 Cal.

What You Need for the Dry Ingredients:

- Ground sesame/poppy seeds - .5 cup
- Flax meal - .5 cup
- Unflavored whey protein/egg white protein powder - .5 cup
- Almond flour – 1 cup
- Dried oregano – 1 tbsp.
- Coconut flour – 1 cup
- Minced garlic – 1 tbsp.
- Cream of tartar – 1 tbsp.
- Erythritol – 1 tbsp.
- Baking soda – 2 tsp.
- Salt – 1 tsp.

What You Need for the Wet Ingredients:

- Large eggs - 2
- Large egg whites - 6
- Coconut oil - extra-virgin is best - 1 tbsp.
- Hot water – 2 cups

How It's Made:

1. Prepare the oven temperature to 350°F.
2. Toss the sesame seeds in a processor and pulse until powdery. Blend in all of the dry components, omitting the coconut flour for now. Mix well.
3. Mix the hot water and eggs together. Add to the dry fixings, mixing well. Gradually combine the coconut flour until you have a dense uniformity.

4. Scoop the dough onto a baking pan - leaving them several inches apart and sprinkle with the poppy/sesame seeds. Bake for 20-30 minutes or until browned.

Italian Seasoning Buns

Servings: 8
Macros: 2 g Net Carbs | 7 g Prot.| 20 g Fat | 26 Cal.

What You Need:

- Eggs – 6
- Flaxseed – 1 tbsp.
- Coconut flour - .5 cup
- Baking soda - .25 tsp
- Melted coconut oil - .5 cup
- Salt – a pinch
- Italian seasoning - .5-1 tsp.

How It's Made:

1. Mix the coconut oil and eggs. Preheat the oven to 350°F.
2. Sift the flour and mix with the baking soda, salt, and Italian seasoning; mixing well until creamy smooth.
3. Leave the dough alone and don't knead it for 5 to 10 minutes. At that time, just shape the dough into buns or bread if you prefer.
4. Prepare a baking tin with a sheet of parchment paper. Arrange the bread on the tin and sprinkle with the flaxseeds. Bake for 30 to 40 minutes and enjoy!

Protein Buns

Servings: 8
Macros: 0.1 g Net Carbs | 6.4 g Prot.| 0.3 g Fat | 29 Cal.

What You Need:

- Eggs – 2
- Water - .5 cup
- Stevia – 1 dash
- Soya protein powder – 1.5 - 2 oz.
- Vanilla extract - .125 tsp.
- Cinnamon – .125 tsp.
- Oil- for the holders

How It's Made:

1. Warm up the oven to reach 425°F. Prepare 8 silicone cups with a spritz of oil. Whisk the eggs and add the rest of the fixings.
2. Portion the batter into the cups and bake for 20 minutes.
3. Lower the setting to 340°F and bake for another 10-15 minutes.
4. Cool on a rack briefly and serve.

Sesame Buns

Servings: 12 buns
Macros: 4 g Net Carbs | 7 g Prot.| 6.5 g Fat | 133 Cal.

What You Need:

- Baking powder – 1 tbsp.
- Sesame seeds - .5 cup (+) .5 cup to cover the buns
- Psyllium powder - .5 cup
- Coconut flour – 1 cup
- Pumpkin seeds - .5 cup
- Hot water – 1 cup
- Sea salt – 1 tbsp.
- Egg whites – 8
- Water – 1 cup boiling

How It's Made:

1. Set the oven in advance to warm up - 350°F.
2. Combine the dry fixings. Blend the egg whites in a blender until foamy. Combine them in a food processor until crumbly.
3. Add the water and stir to create a smoother dough. Make 12 buns.
4. Empty the additional 1/2 cup sesame seeds in a dish and cover the top side of the bun. Arrange the buns on a parchment paper covered cookie sheet. Bake for 50 minutes. For a crunchy top, let the buns cool down in the oven.

Spring Onion Buns

Servings: 6
Macros: 1.1 g Net Carbs | 4.2 g Prot.| 6.7 g Fat | 81 Cal.

What You Need:

- Separated eggs – 3
- Stevia – 1 tsp.
- Cream cheese – 3.5 oz.
- Baking powder - .5 tsp
- Salt – 1 pinch

What You Need for the Filling:

- Chopped hard-boiled egg - 1
- Diced spring onions – 2 sprigs

How It's Made:

1. Preheat the oven to 300°F. Spritz the muffin cups with some oil.
2. Mix the egg yolks, with the stevia, cream cheese, salt, and baking powder.
3. Whisk the egg whites in another cup. Combine the fixings with a spatula and add the dough into six of the muffin cups (1/2 full).
4. Combine the chopped egg with the onions (filling fixings) and add to the cups. Pour more dough into the cup and bake for 30 minutes. Cool slightly and serve. Make sure they are 'totally' cold before storing.

Rolls

Coconut Flour Rolls

Servings: 10
Macros: 1.3 g Net Carbs | 3 g Prot.| 7 g Fat | 102 Cal.

What You Need:

- Coconut flour - .5 cup
- Psyllium husk powder – 2 tbsp.
- Baking powder - .5 tsp.
- Pink Himalayan salt - .25 tsp.
- Water - .75 cup
- Large eggs – 4
- Butter – 4 tbsp.

How It's Made:

1. Place the oven temperature at 350°F.
2. Combine all of the dry fixings (flour, husk powder, salt, and baking powder).
3. In another dish, whisk the eggs with an electric mixer. Pour in the water and melted butter.
4. Slowly, combine by adding the dry into the wet components. Shape into ten dinner rolls and place on a silicone baking mat or greased baking sheet.
5. Bake for 30-35 minutes and serve.

Delicious Dinner Rolls

Servings: 12 rolls
Macros: 3 g Net Carbs | 11 g Prot. | 18.7 g Fat | 221 Cal.

What You Need:

- Mozzarella cheese – 2 cups – 8 oz. pkg.
- Cream cheese – 3 oz.
- Eggs – 2
- Almond flour – 2.5 cups
- Baking powder – 2 tsp.
- Baking soda – 1 tsp.

How It's Made:

1. Add the cheeses into a microwavable dish and melt. Stir in the eggs.
2. In another container, whisk the baking soda, almond flour, and baking powder. Combine all of the fixings. Blend well with your hands.
3. Prepare 12 balls and place on a greased baking pan. Bake until browned to your preference.

Fathead Rolls

Servings: 4 – 2 per serving
Macros: 2.5 g Net Carbs | 7 g Prot.| 13 g Fat | 160 Cal.

What You Need:

- Shredded mozzarella cheese - .75 cup
- Cream cheese – 2 oz. - 4 tbsp.
- Shredded cheddar cheese - .5 cup
- Beaten egg – 1
- Garlic powder - .25 tsp.
- Almond flour - .33 cup
- Baking powder – 2 tsp.

How It's Made:

1. Heat up the oven to 425°F.
2. Combine the mozzarella and cream cheese. Place in the microwave. Cook for about 20 seconds at a time until the cheese melts.
3. In another container, beat the egg and add the dry fixings.
4. Work in the mozzarella. (The dough will be sticky). Stir in cheddar cheese. Scoop the dough into a sheet of plastic wrap. Sprinkle the top of the bread with the almond flour.
5. Fold the plastic wrap over the dough. Gently start working into a ball. Be sure it is covered and place in the fridge for 1/2 hour.
6. Slice the dough ball into four sections and roll each one into a ball. Cut the ball in half (top and bottom of the bun).

7. Place the cut side down onto a well-greased sheet pan. Bake for 10 to 12 minutes. Fix them like you like them.

Keto Bread Rolls

Servings: 6
Macros: 4.7 g Net Carbs | 6.2 g Prot.| 15 g Fat | 203 Cal.

What You Need for the Dry Ingredients:

- Almond flour – 1.25 cups
- Coconut flour - .25 cup
- Ground psyllium husk - .25 cup (+) 3 tbsp.
- Salt - .5 tsp.
- Baking powder – 2 tsp.

What You Need for the Wet Ingredients:

- Apple cider vinegar – 2 tsp.
- Olive – 1 tbsp.
- Hot water - like hot bath temperature – 1 cup

What You Need for the Toppings:

- Sesame seeds – optional – 2 tbsp.

How It's Made:

1. Preheat oven to 375°F. Prepare a baking tray with parchment paper. Set aside for now.
2. In a large mixing container, combine all of the dry fixings first (almond flour, coconut flour, ground psyllium husk, baking powder, and salt). Mix well.
3. Pour in the olive oil and vinegar as well as the hot water. Combine for 1 minute using a spatula. It should remain sticky and soft, but you should be able to form a ball with your hand. If not, just add more

husk (1 tsp. at a time). Don't add more than 1 tablespoon of husk.

4. Set aside 10 minutes to let the fiber absorb the liquid. The dough should be elastic, soft and easy to divide into 6 small balls.

5. Roll each small roll between your hands and arrange them on the baking tray. They will not expand while baking.

6. Brush the top of each bread ball with a little tap water. Sprinkle some sesame seeds on top of each bread for a delicious treat.

7. Warm up the oven to 375F. Bake 40-45 minutes. I recommend you place the tray at the *very bottom* of the oven for 1/2 hour. Then, swap the pan to the *top* level of the oven for 10-15 extra minutes. If you love your bread crusty, turn onto the grill mode for an additional 5 minutes after the baking time. Watch them closely. Thoroughly cool down a wire rack. Slice halfway and enjoy as a bread roll with butter or another tasty treat (add those carbs).

8. Store in the pantry for 5-6 days. You can store it in a towel to keep them fresh. Rewarm them sliced, in the toaster to add some crispiness. You can also freeze the bread and double the recipe to make more in advance.

Low-Carb Cream Cheese Rolls

Servings: 6 rolls
Macros: 0.8 g Net Carbs | 4.2 g Prot.| 8 g Fat | 91.3 Cal.

What You Need:

- Large eggs – 3
- Full-fat cream cheese - cubed & cold – 3 oz.
- Cream of tartar - .125 tsp.
- Salt - .125 tsp.

How It's Made:

1. Warm up the oven to 300°F. Line a baking tin with parchment paper. Spritz the pan with cooking oil spray.
2. Carefully, separate the yolks from the eggs and place the whites in a non-greasy container. Whisk with the tartar until stiff.
3. In another container, whisk the cream cheese, salt, and yolks until smooth.
4. Fold in the whites of the eggs, mixing well using a spatula. Mound a scoop of whites over the yolk mixture and fold together as you rotate the dish. Continue the process until well combined. The process helps to eliminate the air bubbles.
5. Portion six large spoons of the mixture onto the prepared pan. Mash the tops with the spatulate to slightly flatten.
6. Bake until browned (30-40 min.).
7. Cool a few minutes in the pan. Then, carefully arrange them on a wire rack to cool.
8. Store in a zipper-type bag – open slightly – and store in the fridge for a couple of days for best results.

Chapter 9: Crackers & Chips

Crackers

Almond Crackers

Servings: 40 crackers – 10 crackers per serving
Macros: 3 g Net Carbs | 6 g Prot. | 15 g Fat | 173 Cal.

What You Need:

- Almond flour – 1 cup
- Water – 3 tbsp.
- Ground flaxseed – 1 tbsp.
- Fine sea salt - .5 tsp.
- Optional: Flaked sea salt

How It's Made:

1. Warm up the oven to reach 350°F.
2. Prepare the dough by combining the first 4 ingredients. Lay it out on a sheet of parchment paper and cover with a second sheet. Use your hands and a rolling pin to press the dough to about 1/8-inch thickness.
3. Sprinkle with the flaked sea salt – if using. Use a pizza slicer to make the cuts about .5-1-inch sections. Try to use triangular cuts.
4. Arrange on a paper-lined baking pan for 20-25 minutes. Cool completely and enjoy any time. Store in an airtight container.

Butter Crackers

Servings: 25
Macros: 1 g Net Carbs | 2 g Prot. | 8 g Fat |90 Cal.

What You Need:

- Almond flour – 2.25 cups
- Egg whites – 2
- Softened - not melted – salted butter – 8 tbsp.
- Salt – A pinch

How It's Made:

1. Warm up the oven temperature to 350°F.
2. Combine the egg whites, and butter in a mixing container on the low-medium setting using a hand mixer – beating until smooth.
3. Fold in the salt and almond flour – mixing a low speed until well mixed.
4. Place the dough between 2 sheets of parchment and roll out on the baking tin. Score the crackers lightly using a pizza cutter or sharp knife into approximately 1.5-inch squares. Bake for 10-15 minutes. Cool and gently break apart on the scored lines.
5. Storage: They will last up to one week at room temperature. If stored in the fridge, they could lose some of the crunchiness.

Chia Seed Crackers

Servings: 36 crackers
Macros: 0.28 g Net Carbs | 0.88 g Prot. | 2.15 g Fat | 28 Cal.

What You Need:

- Chia seeds, ground - .5 cup
- Shredded cheddar cheese – 3 oz.
- Ice water – 1.25 cups
- Psyllium husk powder – 2 tbsp.
- Olive oil – 2 tbsp.
- Xanthan gum - .25 tsp.
- Garlic powder - .25 tsp.
- Onion powder - .25 tsp.
- Oregano - .25 tsp.
- Paprika - .25 tsp.
- Salt - .25 tsp.
- Pepper - .25 tsp.

How It's Made:

1. Use a spice grinder to prepare the chia seeds and add to the rest of the dry fixings. Warm up the oven to reach 375°F.
2. Blend the oil into the dry components to make a sandy consistency. Add the water into the mixture to form the dough. Fold in the cheddar and mix well. Place on a silpat to rest 5 minutes or so. Roll out the dough until it's thin.
3. Bake for 30 to 35 minutes. Remove and slice into individual crackers.

4. Place back in the oven to broil for 5 to 7 minutes until crispy.

5. Chill and serve or store.

Coconut Almond Crisps

Servings: 12 cookies
Macros: 1.16 g Net Carbs | 0.68g Prot. | 6.12 g Fat | 64 Cal.

What You Need:

- Butter - .25 cup
- Swerve sweetener - .33 cup
- Blackstrap molasses – 2 tsp.
- Xanthan gum - .25 tsp.
- Almond meal - .25 cup
- Shredded coconut – 6 tbsp.
- Vanilla extract - .5 tsp.

How It's Made:

1. Prepare 2 baking tins with parchment paper. Warm up the oven to 350°F.
2. Arrange the oven rack to the uppermost level in the oven.
3. Use medium heat to melt the butter, molasses, and swerve. When combined, remove from the burner and add the xanthan gum. Whisk briskly and work in the shredded coconut, vanilla extract, and almond meal.
4. Use a teaspoon to drop the batter onto the prepared pans (4-in. between). Slightly, press down each one and bake for 8-12 minutes.
5. Once they are golden browned, cool thoroughly in the pan to crisp up.

Cranberry Hazelnut Crisps

Servings: 18 – 64-72 crackers
Macros: 2.8 g Net Carbs | 5.96 g Prot. | 12.87 g Fat | 115 Cal.

What You Need:

- Large organic eggs - 2
- Unsweetened dried cranberries- .5 cup
- Roasted hazelnuts - .5 cup
- Pumpkin seeds - .33 cup
- Almond flour – 3 cups
- Erythritol sweetener - brown sugar version is best - .25 cup
- Baking soda – 2 tsp.
- Salt - .5 tsp.
- Water - .5 - .75 cup
- Apple cider vinegar - 1 tbsp.

How It's Made:

1. Warm up the oven to 350°F. Prepare 4 mini loaf pans with a spritz of oil.
2. Finely chop the hazelnuts, cranberries, and pumpkin seeds. Combine with the sweetener, flour, salt, and baking soda.
3. Stir in the eggs with .5 cup of the water and the vinegar. It should be thick, but it should scoop into the prepared pans. You can add more water if needed (1 tbsp. at a time).
4. Portion into the pans and bake for 30-35 minutes. They should be firm when touched. Let the bread cool in the

pans. Place in the freezer for at least one hour – maybe two hours - before slicing.

5. Heat up the oven to 250°F and line baking sheets with a sheet of parchment paper. Slice the bread (no more than .25-inch thick). Bake until browned (20-30 min.), and firm to touch. Let the crisps stay in the oven to cool.

6. Tip: If the crisps become softened, place them in a preheated 200°F oven for about 20 minutes.

Goat Cheese Crackers

Servings: 12

Macros: 2 g Net Carbs | 3 g Prot.| 8 g Fat | 99 Cal.

What You Need:

- Baking powder – 1 tsp.
- Fresh rosemary – 2 tbsp.
- Butter – 4 tbsp.
- Coconut flour - .5 cup.
- Goat cheese – 6 oz.

How It's Made:

1. Preheat the oven to reach 380°F.
2. Use a food processor to mix all of the components, processing until creamy smooth.
3. Roll the dough out using a rolling pin until it's about .25-.5-inches thick. Use a cookie cutter or knife to portion the crackers.
4. Place on a parchment paper-lined pan and bake for 15-20 minutes.

Graham Crackers

Servings: 24
Macros: 1 g Net Carbs | 6 g Fat| 1 g Protein | 71 Cal.

What You Need:

- Baking soda - .5 tsp.
- Almond flour – 2 cups
- Xanthan gum - .5 tsp or Flax meal – 1 tsp.
- Kosher salt - .25 tsp.
- Ground cinnamon – 1 tsp.
- Butter at room temperature - 5.5 tbsp.
- Golden erythritol – 6 tbsp. or Pyure - 3 tbsp.
- Egg - 1

How It's Made:

1. Combine the baking soda, flour, salt, cinnamon, and xanthan gum into a mixing container and thoroughly mix. Put to the side.
2. Cream the butter for 2-3 minutes using an electric mixer. Mix in the sweetener. Continue beating until light, and much of the sweetener has liquified.
3. Stir in egg, mixing until just mixed. On low, use the mixer and add in half of your flour mixture- mixing until just incorporated. Mix in the rest.
4. Wrap the dough in plastic. Place in the fridge for a minimum of one hour - up to three days.
5. When ready to bake, warm up the oven to reach 350°F.
6. Roll out the dough until thin. Use a pastry cutter to cut the dough into squares. Place on a parchment paper-lined tray. Store in the freezer for 10 minutes before baking.

7. Bake for 8 to 12 minutes - depending on the thickness and size.
8. Be sure to leave them in the pan for 10 minutes before transferring to a cooling rack. You can store in a closed dish for up to five days.

Hemp Heart Crackers

Servings: 36
Macros: 1 g Net Carbs | 1 g Prot. | 6 g Fat | 76 Cal.

What You Need:

- Almond flour – 1 cup
- Coconut flour - .5 cup (+) more for prepping the dough
- Hemp hearts - .5 cup
- Baking powder – 3 tsp.
- Optional: Xanthan gum - 1 tsp.
- Salt for topping - .5 tsp.
- Baking soda - .25 tsp.
- Salted butter – very cold – 6 tbsp.
- Melted butter with salt – 4 tbsp.
- Olive oil – 2 tbsp.
- Ice water - .66 cup

How It's Made:

1. Warm up the oven to 400°F
2. Put the hemp hearts, almond flour, baking soda, coconut flour, baking powder, and salt in a mixing container – mixing well.
3. Grate the chilled butter, stirring it into the flour mixture.
4. Pour in the olive oil. Stir until all of the olive oil is blended into the flour mixture and add the water. Place the dough in the fridge for at least 30 minutes.
5. At that time, dust a silpat or sheet of parchment with coconut flour.
6. Prepare the dough (1/4-inch thickness), and dust with flour. Cut into the desired shapes.

7. You can use a toothpick to poke holes in the crackers. Bake for 15-20 minutes.
8. Prepare the butter with .5 tsp. of salt to brush the crackers while they are hot. Turn oven off and put the tray back in the oven for five minutes. Remove and cool the batch entirely before storing.

Pesto Crackers

Servings: 6
Macros: 2.96 g Net Carbs | 5.34 g Prot. | 19.3 g Fat | 204.5 Cal.

What You Need:

- Almond flour – 1.25 cups
- Ground black pepper - .25 tsp.
- Salt - .5 tsp.
- Baking powder - .5 tsp.
- Dried basil - .25 tsp.
- Cayenne pepper – 1 pinch
- Pressed clove of garlic - 1
- Basil pesto – 2 tbsp.
- Butter – 3 tbsp.

How It's Made:

1. Warm up the oven to reach 325°F. Line a cookie sheet with a sheet of parchment paper.
2. Whisk the baking powder, salt, flour, and pepper. Toss in the cayenne, garlic, and basil. Stir in the pesto and form a dough mixture.
3. Fold in the butter with your fingers or a fork until a dough ball is formed.
4. Arrange on the baking sheet and spread it out until thin. Bake for 14-17 minutes. Remove from the oven, and cut into crackers.

Toasted Sesame Crackers

Servings: 6
Macros: 3 g Net Carbs | 11 g Prot.| 17 g Fat | 213 Cal.

What You Need:

- Toasted sesame seeds – .25 cup
- Almond flour – 1 cup
- Grated asiago cheese – .5 cup
- Egg white – 1
- Dijon mustard – 1 tbsp.
- Salt – .5 tsp.
- Paprika – 1 tsp.

How It's Made:

1. Warm up the oven until it reaches 325°F. Lightly grease a sheet of foil in a baking pan.
2. Combine all of the fixings except for the salt into a blender or processor. Pulse until it shapes into dough.
3. Take it from the processor and roll out the dough to form a log (1.5 in. round). Slice them into 1/4-inch slices.
4. Arrange on the baking sheet and sprinkle with the salt.
5. Bake for 17 to 20 minutes.

Unflavored Coconut Flour Muffins

Servings: 1
Macros: 5 g Net Carbs | 7 g Prot. | 6 g Fat | 113 Cal.

What You Need:

- Eggs – 1
- Baking powder - .25 tsp.
- Coconut flour – 2 tsp.
- Salt - pinch

How It's Made:

1. Sift the flour and combine all of the fixings.
2. Warm up the oven to 400°F.
3. Grease the muffin cups and add the mixture.
4. Bake for 12 minutes and serve or cool to store.

Tortillas & Chips
Flax Tortillas

Servings: 5
Macros: 2.18 g Net Carbs | 4.99 g Prot.| 11.78 g Fat | 184.4 Cal.

What You Need:

- Golden flaxseed meal – 1 cup
- Psyllium husk powder – 2 tbsp.
- Olive oil – 2 tsp.
- Xanthan gum - .25 tsp.
- Curry powder - .5 tsp.
- Filtered water - 1 cup (+) 2 tbsp.

What You Need Per Tortilla:

- Olive oil - for frying – 1 tsp
- Coconut flour - for rolling - .5 tsp.

How It's Made:

1. Combine all of the dry fixings and add 2 teaspoons of oil and the water. Mix to form a dough. Let it rest uncovered for one hour on the countertop.
2. If cutting by hand, cut into 3 blocks. If you have a tortilla press, spit it into 5 chunks.
3. Press each portion with your hand and sprinkle with the coconut flour. Roll them out as thin as possible. Use a glass to cut out the tortillas. Re-roll any extra dough pieces.
4. Warm up the oil for frying and simmer over med-high heat for each of the tortillas.

Conclusion

I hope you have enjoyed each segment of *Keto Bread*. I hope it was informative and provided you with all of the tools you need to achieve your goals whatever they may be. If you are attempting to drop the pounds, you need to keep it simple and drink plenty of water. You can also flavor your drinks using stevia-based flavorings or lemon juice. Consider some of these drink choices. This is calculated with your grams of carbs derived for you.

- Water with lemon: 0
- Water: 0
- Tea 0 – Add 1 sugar cube = 4 grams
- Coffee 0
- Diet soft drink 0 – Beware of artificial sweeteners
- 1 cup coconut water: 9
- 1 cup soy milk: 12
- 1 cup orange juice: 26
- 8 oz. unsweetened almond milk: 2

Enjoy Coffee & Tea: If you are struggling during your dieting plan, it is always good to know you can enjoy black coffee and unsweetened tea for -0- net carbs. It is best to choose fresh organic milk products. You can also add additional protein and calcium using non-dairy products such as cashew or almond milk.

Lastly, do you know how to read an ingredient list when you are doing your shopping? This is one crucial element as you do your grocery shopping while on your ketogenic diet plan. The FDA requires food manufacturers to list the components in each product sold in order of weight predominance. Check the first five ingredients to ensure they do not have any of the avoided food items.

Recall how to calculate your carbs. You take the total carbohydrates minus the dietary fiber and minus sugar alcohol (if any) to equal the Net Carbs.

All you need to do now is prepare a shopping list of all of the items you want to make for a couple of days. You don't have to stick to the daily plan as it is described, but you do need to remember to count all carbs. You can mix and match as long as you stay within the limitations of your chosen method.

Stay determined by your goals during your transition to ketosis. Follow the instructions and recipe methods. Before long, you will be able to quickly scan other recipes and know before you finish reading how healthy they are for you and your family.

Enjoy your new way of preparing your baked goods, and before you realize it, your family will be enjoying each and every recipe found in your new *Keto Bread Cookbook*.

Index for the Recipes

Chapter 3: Bread & Biscuits

Bread

Almond Bread
Cheesy Italian Baked Bread
Cloud Bread
Coconut Bread
Cottage Bread
Flax Bread
Flaxseed Bread with Coconut Flour
Garlic Bread with Cheese – Slow-Cooked
Garlic & Cheese Monkey Bread
Gluten-Free Bread
Keto Bread Loaves
Low-Carb Cream Cheese Bread
Macadamia Bread
Microwave Bread
Paleo Bread – Keto Style
Sesame Seed Bread
Spring Onion Bread
Stuffed Savory Bread

Sweet Bread

Banana Bread
Cinnabons
Coconut Balls
Gingerbread – Slow-Cooked
Lemon & Blueberry Bread
Pumpkin Bread
Seedy Pumpkin Bread

Ham and Apple Flatbread
Matzo Bread
Pita Bread

Tart Pie Crust

Chapter 6: Muffins

Apple & Almond Muffins
Bacon & Asparagus Muffins
Bacon & Cheese Cauliflower Muffins
Brownie Muffins
Cheeseburger Muffin Buns
Cinnamon & Apple Spiced Muffins
Cinnamon & Applesauce Muffins
Eggplant Muffins
English Muffins
Ham Muffins
Lemon Coconut Muffins
Lemon Poppyseed Muffins
Pesto Egg Muffins
Pistachio Muffins
Pumpkin Muffins
Pumpkin Maple Flaxseed Muffins
Squash Muffins

Chapter 7: Bagels

Bagels with Cheese
Everything Bagels
Bagel Seasoning
Cheesy Bagels
Cinnamon Raisin Bagels
Croissant Bagels
Garlic Coconut Flour Gluten-Free Bagels

Mozzarella Bagels
Onion Bagels – Gluten-Free
Pumpkin Bagels

Chapter 8: Buns & Rolls

Buns

Basil Buns
Breakfast Buns
Buns for Burgers
Italian Seasoning Buns
Protein Buns
Sesame Buns
Spring Onion Buns

Rolls

Coconut Flour Rolls
Delicious Dinner Rolls
Fathead Rolls
Keto Bread Rolls
Low-Carb Cream Cheese Rolls

Chapter 9: Crackers & Chips

Crackers

Almond Crackers
Butter Crackers
Chia Seed Crackers
Coconut Almond Crisps
Cranberry Hazelnut Crisps
Goat Cheese Crackers

Graham Crackers
Hemp Heart Crackers
Pesto Crackers
Toasted Sesame Crackers
Unflavored Coconut Flour Muffins

Tortillas

Flax Tortillas

Book II: Keto Desserts

Table of Contents

Introduction

I am so excited that you have chosen to take a new path using the Ketogenic diet with the aid of the *Keto Desserts*. The following chapters will discuss how to follow the plan and the ways it will most benefit your health. If you take the approach of eating less without considering your diet, you could be losing essential minerals and vitamins you need daily. Unfortunately, this can result in muscle spasms, fatigue, mental fogginess, hunger, headaches, irritability, insomnia, and emotional depression. You can also lose valuable muscle mass—not just the pounds you intended to drop. The lifestyle change is worth the journey.

Stages of the Ketogenic Plan

This is an important step. You must decide how you want to proceed with your diet plan. It is always best to discuss this with your physician. These are the basics:

Method 1: Choose from the standard Ketogenic diet (SKD) which consists of high fat, moderate protein, and extremely low carbs.

Method 2: The cyclical Ketogenic diet (CKD) is created with 5 Keto days followed by 2 high-carbohydrate days.

Method 3: The high-protein Keto (HPK) diet is much like the SKD plan in all aspects, except that it has more protein.

Method 4: The targeted Keto diet (TKD) will provide you with a plan to add carbs to the diet during the times when you are working out.

If you are new to the Ketogenic way of eating, you will probably want to use the first method. You can range from 20 to 50 calories in one day. Hence, you may want to use your carbs wisely. Each of the recipes in this cookbook is calculated so that you will understand how much you can indulge with the delicious treats.

Before we get started, why not try a cup of Butter Coffee? Here is the Recipe:

Servings: 1

Macros: 0 g Net Carbs | 0 g Protein | 25 g Fat | 230 Cal.

Ingredients:

- Coffee – 2 tbsp.
- Water – 1 cup
- Grass-fed butter – 1 tbsp.
- Coconut oil – 1 tbsp.
- Useful: Turkish coffee pot or a regular pot

Preparation Method:

1. Prepare your coffee the way you like it. You can simmer ground coffee in water for five minutes and strain it into the cup.
2. Pour the coffee into a high-speed blender (for example – NutriBullet). Add the coconut, oil, and butter. Mix for about 10 seconds.
3. Pour it into a mug and relax. Add cinnamon or whipped cream (but count the carbs), and enjoy!

Now, that is just for starters. Just sit back and relax. If you are new to the diet plan, the first chapter will enlighten you for the basics. If you are a veteran, maybe there is something there for you as well.

Chapter 1: Essentials of the Ketogenic Diet

Just to get you on the right track for preparing your delicious desserts and special treats, this section will provide you a few essential guidelines.

The "Yes" Foods

To supplement your Ketogenic diet plan, refer to the following list. It will provide you with an abundance of "sweet" food choices included on the Keto diet. Experiment with your new recipes, and use this list as a guideline when you begin your dessert planning list:

Fats & Oils: Plan your fats from natural sources including nuts. It is best to supplement with saturated and monounsaturated fats—including butter, extra-virgin olive oil (EVOO), and similar items you will see throughout the diet plan cookbook.

Dairy Products: Choose dairy products that have been cultured and are Keto-friendly. Milk alone is high in carbs (lactose), unless its cultured and turned into the sour cream for example. You can also try dairy substitutes. The number one choice is unsweetened almond milk. You can also choose from hemp milk and flax milk.

Do you know the difference between butter and ghee? Butter consists of water, milk solids, and butterfat. On the other hand, ghee, an Indian staple, includes pure butterfat. Therefore, if you have lactose sensitivities, ghee is probably your best choice. The ghee also contains medium chain fatty acids, which assist your immune system and digestion.

Nuts & Seeds: Create some tasty meals (in moderation) when adding seeds and nuts to your Keto diet plan. Use fattier nuts including macadamias and almonds.

Lemon and Lime: Your blood sugar levels will naturally drop with these citric additions and signal a boost in your liver function. The choices are limitless and assist you with the following:

- Relieves respiratory infections
- Reduces toothache pain
- Boosts your immune system
- Balances pH
- Reduces fever
- Excellent for weight loss
- Blood purifier
- Decreases wrinkles and blemishes

Cinnamon: Use cinnamon as part of your daily plan to improve your insulin receptor activity. Just put one-half of a teaspoon of cinnamon into a shake or any type of Keto dessert. As you will see, many of the Keto recipes contain the ingredient.

A Note About Pumpkin: Include pumpkin in your 'must have' list even though it is considered a vegetable. It is full of essential minerals and vitamins including B1, B6, and PP. Carotenes are also in abundance with vitamin A. It has been noted that pumpkin is about 4.5 times higher in vitamin A than carrots. You will notice many of the dessert recipes will incorporate pumpkin into its list.

Low Carb Flours: As you begin your new and healthier lifestyle, you will discover many shortcuts or substitutes to help you stay on track. Some of these replacements will help:

- **Almond Flour:** Almond flour is more of an all-purpose flour and only contains 3 grams of carbs for 1/4 of a cup. (In comparison, totals are overwhelming for the regular wheat flour at 24 grams. This is why it is not on your diet plan!) almonds are blanched in boiling water to remove the skins and then ground into a fine flour used for baking low-carb cakes, cookies and pie crusts.

- **Almond Meal**: Almond meal isn't the same as almond flour. If you are running low on almond flour for baked goods like muffins and cookies, then merely throw some almonds in a food processor to make some almond meal.

- **Coconut Flour:** Each 1/4 cup of coconut flour contains 19 g of carbohydrates, 6 g of protein, 60 calories, 2.5 g of fat, 12 g of fiber, and 7 g of net carbs. It displays that tropical taste. Be sure it's stored in a closed container. Choose a spot where it's dark such as the pantry. The refrigerator and freezer could cause moisture contamination.

- **Ground Psyllium Husk Powder:** You will find this in several recipes. It is a binding agent with tons of fiber.

Low-Carb Sweeteners: Consider these choices:

- **Stevia Drops** include hazelnut, vanilla, English toffee, and chocolate flavors. Enjoy making a satisfying cup of sweetened coffee or other favorite drink. Some individuals think the drops are too bitter. At first, use only three drops to equal one teaspoon of sugar.

- **Swerve Granular Sweetener** is also an excellent choice as a blend. It's made from non-digestible carbs sourced from starchy root veggies and select fruits. Give it a try if you don't like the taste of stevia. Start with 3/4 of a teaspoon for every one of sugar. Increase the portion to your liking. Swerve also has its own confectioners or powdered sugar for your baking needs. On the downside, it is more expensive. You have to decide if it's worth the difference.

- **Xylitol** is at the top of the sugary list. It tastes just like sugar! The natural occurring sugar alcohol has the Glycemic index (GI) standing of 13. If you have tried others and weren't satisfied, this might be for you. Xylitol is also known to keep mouth bacteria in check which goes a long way to protect your dental health. The ingredient is commonly found in chewing gum. Unfortunately, if used in large amounts, it can cause diarrhea – making chewing gum a laxative if used in large quantities. *Pet Warning*: If you have a puppy in the house, be sure to use caution since it is toxic to dogs (even small amounts).

Chocolate: Dark chocolate is the best type for your Ketogenic diet. Sugar-free and the darker it is – the better. It is used in many of the following recipes.

Your Basic Shopping List

Take extra time to get organized before you begin your new diet plan. The items included in this segment will provide an excellent base stock for your menu planning needs. Store and clearly mark all food items that are used at the time the dessert is planned. All you need to do is count the carbs to remain in Ketosis. Each of the categories provides you with examples of the stock:

Pantry Items

These are some of the favorites for your baking and preparation of desserts while on the Ketogenic diet:

- Coconut flour
- Stevia
- Sugar-free gelatin
- Unsweetened cocoa powder
- Natural nut butter – no sugar

Dairy Products

It is essential to maintain your health using dairy products. It is best to choose fresh organic milk products. You can also add additional protein and calcium using non-dairy products such as cashew or almond milk. Keep these in the fridge:

- Heavy cream
- Butter
- Cream cheese
- Sour cream

- Ghee
- Parmesan cheese
- Sharp cheddar cheese

Healthy Fats

To achieve success in the Ketogenic diet, you need fats. These are some of those:

- Avocado
- Extra-virgin olive oil (EVOO)
- Sesame, avocado, and coconut oil
- Flaxseed oil
- Coconut flakes
- Olives

The Foods to *Avoid*

There are many healthy options to choose from while on the Ketogenic diet. Avoid the foods in the following groups – unless they are structured within this cookbook or other professional sources you trust. Each dessert item has been calculated with all of the nutritional information and servings listed.

- **Regular Dairy Milk**: Avoid regular milk for sure since it packs almost 13 grams of carbohydrates per cup.

- **Added Sugars**: The sugars to avoid include honey, maltose, dextrose, corn syrup, and maltodextrin.

- **Artificial Sweeteners**: Several types to avoid include saccharin, sucralose, and Splenda.

Benefits of MCT Oils

Your Ketogenic experience can improve with the use of MCT oil or medium chain triglycerides. These unique fatty acids are found in a natural form in palm and coconut oil. You will notice some of the smoothies use this as a component. These are just a few of the examples:

- The oil helps lower your blood sugar.
- The use of MCTs makes it much easier to get into – and remain – in Ketosis.
- It is a natural anti-convulsive.
- It is also excellent for appetite control and weight loss.

Important Note: Seek your doctor's advice before changing your eating patterns. In some cases, you could reduce the need for some medications.

Tools & Equipment

Each of these tools will help you speed up the baking process with your chosen dessert items.

Tool 1: Scales: It is almost a necessity to own a set of food scales to take out the guesswork. Keep this information in mind before you make the purchase:

- Seek a Conversion Button: You need to know how to convert measurements into grams since not all recipes have them listed. The grams keep the system in complete harmony.

- The Tare Function: When you set a bowl on the scale, the feature will allow you to reset the scale back to zero (0).

- Removable Plate: Keep the germs off the scale by removing the plate. Be sure it will come off to eliminate the bacterial buildup.

Tool 2: Food Processor, Immersion Blender or Regular Blender: Each of these will be an essential part of preparing many of the recipes for desserts.

Tool 3: Slow Cooker or Crockpot: You will find the crockpot a must if you have a busy lifestyle. These are just a couple of ways you can benefit from its use:

- Save a lot of Effort and Time: All it takes is a few good recipes and a little bit of your valuable time. In most of the cases, these recipes are geared towards a fast lifestyle and will be ready with just a few simple steps. After some time and practice, you will know which ones will be your favorites.

- Get Ahead of the Meal: Preparing food with your slow cooker can put you ahead of the game. You can prepare the cooker the night before if you have a busy day planned. All it takes is a few minutes of preparation. Just add all of the fixings into the pot and place it in the fridge – overnight. The next morning, transfer to the counter to become room temperature. Turn it on as you head out of the door and your dessert will be ready when you get home.

Tool 4: **Accurate Measuring Tools**: A measuring cup and spoon system that shows both the Metric and US standards of weight is essential, so there is no confusion during prep.

A Final Note: Some recipes might not be 100 % Keto-friendly. You can also adjust the ingredients to your own discretion. Remember this Formula: Total Carbs minus (-) Fiber = Net Carbs.

Puddings

Nothing is handier for a treat than an individual fat bomb or a delicious candy choice. If you want something for a mid-morning choice, just try one of these healthy puddings.

Almond Blackberry Chia Pudding

Servings: 2

Macros: 1 g Net Carbs | 2 g Prot. | 8 g Fat | 109 Cal.

Ingredients:

- Fresh blackberries – 6 oz.
- Chia seeds – .25 cup
- Raw honey – 1 drizzle to taste
- Vanilla almond milk – 1.5 cups
- Sliced almonds – 2-3 tbsp.

Preparation Method:

1. Toss the berries into a dish, and crush with a fork until creamy.
2. Fold in a drizzle of honey, milk, and chia seeds. Stir well.
3. Refrigerate for several hours or overnight for best results.
4. Sprinkle with the almonds and several blackberries.
5. Serve and enjoy anytime.

Almond Pumpkin Pudding

Servings: 10

Macros: 4 g Net Carbs | 6 g Prot. | 16 g Fat | 154 Cal.

Ingredients:

- Coconut oil – 5 oz.
- Pumpkin puree – 10 oz.
- Coconut cream – 5 oz.
- Pumpkin pie spice – 1 tbsp.
- Powdered Erythritol – 3 tbsp.
- Almonds – 4 oz.
- Ginger – .75 tsp.

Preparation Method:

1. Combine and stir all of the fixings (omit the almonds) in a saucepan using the medium heat setting (10 min.).
2. Pour into silicone molds and press an almond inside each one.
3. Freeze for a minimum of one hour. Then you can remove from the molds and serve or freeze for later.
4. For a taste change, just squeeze a little lemon juice over the pudding before serving.

Cheesecake Pudding

Servings: 6 if you add berries or 4 without

Macros: 5 g Net Carbs | 5 g Prot. | 36 g Fat | 356 Cal.

Ingredients:

- Cream cheese or Neufchatel cheese – 1 block
- Heavy whipping cream – .5 cup
- Lemon juice – 1 tsp.
- Sour cream – .5 cup
- Liquid stevia – 20 drops
- Vanilla extract – 1 tsp.

Preparation Method:

1. Microwave the cream cheese for 30 seconds or leave on the counter to soften for a few minutes before using.
2. Whip the sour cream and whipping cream together with a hand mixer until soft peaks form. Combine with the rest of the fixings and whip until fluffy.
3. Portion into four dishes to chill. Cover with plastic wrap in the fridge.
4. When ready to eat, garnish with some berries if you like.
5. Please remember; if you add the berries, add the carbs.

Chocolate Avocado Pudding

Servings: 2

Macros: 2 g Net Carbs | 27 g Fat | 8 g Prot. | 281 Cal.

Ingredients:

- Room temperature cream cheese – 2 oz.
- Ripe medium avocado – 1
- Natural sweetener – swerve – 1 tsp.
- Vanilla extract – .25 tsp.
- Unsweetened cocoa powder – 4 tbsp.
- Pink salt – 1 pinch

Preparation Method:

1. Combine the cream cheese with the avocado, sweetener, vanilla, cocoa powder, and salt. Add to a blender or processor.
2. Pulse until creamy smooth.
3. Measure into a fancy dessert dishes and chill for at least 30 minutes.

Chocolate Hazelnut Avocado Mousse

Servings: 4
Macros: 4.6 g Net Carbs | 5.5 g Prot. | 25.6 g Fat | 280 Cal.

Ingredients:

- Avocados 14.1 oz – 1 Large
- Raw cacao powder *or* Dutch-process cocoa powder – 4 tbsp.
- Hazelnut butter – 4 tbsp.
- Sugar-free vanilla extract – .5 tsp.
- Powdered Swerve *or* Erythritol – 2 tbsp.
- Stevia extract – 10 drops
- Unsweetened almond milk/cashew milk/coconut milk – 4 tbsp. or 2 fl. oz.
- *Optional Topping:* Chopped dark chocolate & Roasted chopped hazelnuts
- Also Needed: 4-single serving mason jars (5 oz. ea.).

Preparation Method:

1. Combine each of the fixings into a food processor (omit the milk).
2. Blend well, then, add the milk slowly until it's like you prefer.
3. Portion into the jars. Chill in the refrigerator for at least 15 minutes.
4. They will be good for up to 3 days if covered in an air-tight container the refrigerator.

Chocolate Mousse

Servings: 2

Macros: 4 g Net Carbs | 4 g Prot. | 50 g Fat | 460 Cal.

Ingredients:

- Heavy whipping cream – 1.5 tbsp.
- Swerve or another natural sweetener – 1 tbsp.
- Unsweetened cocoa powder – 1 tbsp.
- Butter – 4 tbsp.
- Cream Cheese – 4 tbsp.

Preparation Method:

1. Take the cream cheese and butter out of the refrigerator to become room temperature. Chill a bowl and whisk the cream. Store in the fridge.
2. In another dish, use a hand mixer to combine the sweetener, cream cheese, cocoa powder, and butter until well mixed.
3. Take out the refrigerated cream and fold into the chocolate mixture using a rubber scraper.
4. Portion into two dessert dishes and chill for one hour.

Cinnamon Roll Mousse

Servings: 4

Macros: 5.1 g Net Carbs | 29.3 g Fat | 4.6 g Prot. | 291 Cal.

Ingredients:

- Heavy whipping cream – .5 cup
- Softened full-fat cream cheese – 4.2 oz.
- Powdered Swerve or Erythritol – .25 cup
- Unsalted cashew butter or almond butter – 2 tbsp.
- Cinnamon – 1 tsp.
- Sugar-free vanilla extract – .5 tsp

Ingredients for the Drizzle:

- Coconut butter – 2 tbsp.
- Swerve or Erythritol – 1 tbsp.
- Virgin coconut oil – 1 tsp.
- Also Needed: 4 mason jars

Preparation Method:

1. Combine the heavy cream and cream cheese until smooth. Toss in the rest of the fixings (sweetener to taste).

2. In another container, combine the drizzle components and place in the microwave. Using 10-second intervals, warm it up until it is syrupy.

3. Portion the mouse in the jars and drizzle with the syrup. Dust with some cinnamon and enjoy! It's good for up to five days in the fridge.

Keto Chia Pudding

Servings: 4

Macros: 12 g Net Carbs | 5 g Prot. | 24 g Fat | 273 Cal.

Ingredients:

- Whole ripe avocado – 1
- Chia seeds – .25 cup
- Medium dates – 2
- Almond or coconut milk – 1 cup
- Vanilla extract – .5 tsp.

Preparation Method:

1. Pour the milk, vanilla, avocado, and dates into a blender.
2. Blend until well mixed. Empty over the chia seeds and cover overnight in the refrigerator when you go to bed. You can also let it rest for two to four hours before serving.

Lemon Custard – Slow Cooker

Servings: 4

Macros: 3 g Net Carbs | 7 g Prot. | 30 g Fat | 319 Cal.

Ingredients:

- Fresh lemon juice – .25 cup
- Large egg yolks – 5
- Lemon zest – 1 tbsp.
- Liquid stevia – .5 tsp.
- Vanilla extract – 1 tsp.
- Coconut cream/whipping cream – 2 cups
- Optional: Whipped coconut cream
- Also Needed: Ramekins/4 small jars

Preparation Method:

1. Whisk the liquid stevia, egg yolks, lemon juice, lemon zest, and vanilla. Whip in the heavy cream. Divide into the four jars.
2. Add a rack in the cooker and arrange the jars on top of it. Add water to fill half of the way up the sides of the ramekins.
3. Secure the lid and cook three hours on low.
4. Transfer the jars from the cooker and cool to room temperature. Chill in the fridge approximately three hours.
5. Serve with the whipped cream if desired.

Pumpkin Custard – Crockpot

Servings: 6

Macros: 3 g Net Carbs | 5 g Prot. | 12 g Fat | 147 Cal.

Ingredients:

- Large eggs – 4
- Granulated stevia/Erythritol blend – .5 cup
- Sea salt – .125 tsp.
- Vanilla extract – 1 tsp.
- Pumpkin pie spice – 1 tsp.
- Butter/coconut oil/ghee – 4 tbsp.
- Pumpkin puree Canned or homemade – 1 tsp.
- Super-fine almond flour – .5 cup
- Recommended Size for the Cooker: 3-4-quarts
- Coconut cooking oil spray or butter for the pot

Preparation Method:

1. Take the butter out of the refrigerator to become room temperature. Lightly grease or spray the cooker.
2. Use a mixer to whisk the eggs – blending until smooth. Slowly, add the sweetener.
3. Blend in the vanilla extract and puree. Fold in the pie spice, salt, and almond flour. Mix everything well and add to the crockpot.
4. Secure the lid – with a paper towel between the top and the fixings to absorb moisture on top of the custard.

5. Cook for 2 to 2.75 hours on the low setting. When it's done, it will begin to pull away from the slow cooker. The center will be set.

6. Enjoy warm and top it off with garnishes as desired.

Candy

Chocolate Bonbons

Servings: 6

Macros: -0- g Net Carbs | 1 g Prot. | 10 g Fat | 100 Cal.

Ingredients:

- Butter – 5 tbsp.
- Coconut oil – 3 tbsp.
- Sugar-free raspberry syrup – 2 tbsp.
- Cocoa powder – 2 tbsp.

Preparation Method:

1. Mix the entire batch of ingredients in a pan.
2. Empty the bombs into six molds or muffin tins.
3. Place the prepared tin into the freezer for a minimum of two hours. Enjoy!

Chocolate Coconut Bites

Servings: 6

Macros: 9 g Net Carbs | 9 g Prot. | 27 g Fat | 326 Cal.

Ingredients:

- Unsweetened 80% or higher dark chocolate – 4 oz.
- Heavy cream – .33 cup
- Coconut flour – 1 cup
- Chocolate protein powder – 1 tbsp.
- Shredded unsweetened coconut – .25 cup
- Coconut oil – 4 tbsp.

Preparation Method:

1. Dice the dark chocolate into bits.
2. Warm up the heavy cream in a saucepan (med-low). Stir in the chocolate bits and oil. Continue stirring until combined and remove from the burner.
3. Stir in the protein powder and coconut flour. Store in the refrigerator for a minimum of two hours.
4. Take the dough out of the fridge when they are cool. Shape into balls and roll through the shredded coconut until coated.
5. Store in the fridge in a closed container.

Chocolate Covered Almonds

Servings: 1

Macros: 3 g Net Carbs | 4 g Prot. | 15 g Fat | 183 Cal.

Ingredients:

- Unsweetened dark chocolate baking chips – .75 cup
- Whole raw almonds – 1.5 cups
- Pure vanilla extract – 1 tsp.
- Sea salt – 1 pinch

Preparation Method:

1. Cut a piece of parchment paper and cover a baking tray.
2. Toss the chips into a saucepan using low heat. Stir and add the vanilla.
3. Once the chocolate is melted, add the almonds and stir until coated.
4. Arrange them on the baking tin and dust with the salt.
5. Place in the fridge for a minimum of 30 minutes before you are ready to devour your portion.
6. For a taste change, sprinkle with some ground cinnamon.

Coconut Peanut Butter Balls

Servings: 15

Macros: 0.92 g Net Carbs | 0.98 g Prot. | 3.19 g Fat | 35.1 Cal.

Ingredients:

- Creamy peanut butter – Keto-friendly – 3 tbsp.
- Powdered Erythritol – 2.5 tsp.
- Unsweetened cocoa powder – 3 tsp.
- Almond flour – 2 tsp.
- Unsweetened coconut flakes – .5 cup

Preparation Method:

1. Combine the peanut butter, Erythritol, cocoa, and flour. Place in the freezer for one hour.
2. Spoon out a small spoon size of the butter mix. Roll into the flakes until it is covered.
3. Refrigerate overnight for the best results and enjoy.

Cream Cheese Truffles – Party Time

Servings: 24

Macros: 1.67 g Net Carbs | 1.23 g Prot. | 7 g Fat | 72.7 Cal.

Ingredients:

- Cream cheese, softened – 16 oz.
- Unsweetened cocoa powder – divided – .5 cup
- Swerve confectioners – 4 tbsp.
- Liquid Stevia – .25 tsp.
- Rum extract – .5 tsp.
- Instant coffee – 1 tbsp.
- Water – 2 tbsp.
- Heavy whipping cream – 1 tbsp.
- Paper candy cups for serving – 24

Preparation Method:

1. Combine all of the fixings (set aside 1/4 cup of cocoa powder). Blend well with a hand mixer. Chill in the fridge for about 30 minutes.
2. Dust the countertop with the rest of the cocoa powder. Roll out heaping tablespoons of the mixture in your hands to form about 24 balls.
3. Roll the balls through the powder and place into individual candy cups.
4. Chill for another hour before serving.

Crust-less Cheesecake Bites

Servings: 4

Macros: 2 g Net Carbs | 5 g Prot. | 15 g Fat | 169 Cal.

Ingredients:

- Large eggs – 2
- Sour cream – .25 cup
- Vanilla extract – .25 tsp.
- Room temperature cream cheese – 4 oz.
- Natural sweetener – ex. swerve – .33 cup

Preparation Method:

1. Warm up the oven to reach 350°F. Use a hand mixer to combine the ingredients.
2. Prepare a cupcake pan with 4 disposable paper cups or silicone liners.
3. Fill the cups and bake for 30 minutes.
4. After cooling about 3 hours, serve and enjoy.
5. You can save the extras for up to 3 months if stored in zip-lock type bags.

Macaroons

Servings: 1

Macros: 4 g Net Carbs | 2 g Prot. | 10 g Fat | 90 Cal.

Ingredients:

- Egg whites – 4
- Vanilla – 1 tsp.
- Artificial sweetener of choice – 1 cup
- Water – 4.5 tsp.
- Unsweetened coconut – .5 cup

Preparation Method:

1. Warm up the oven to 325°F.
2. Whisk the eggs with the liquid components. Stir in the coconut and mix.
   Use an immersion blender for uniform consistency.

3. Add the batter into the greased pan and bake for 15 minutes. Enjoy!

No-Bake Chocolate Fudge Haystacks

Servings: 12

Macros: 1.5 g Net Carbs | 2 g Prot. | 18 g Fat | 172 Cal.

Ingredients:

- Softened cream cheese – 4 oz.
- Erythritol sweetener – .75 cup
- Softened unsalted butter – .5 cup
- Unsweetened cocoa powder – .25 cup
- Coarse sea salt – .125 tsp.
- Unsweetened desiccated/shredded coconut – 1 cup
- Sugar-free vanilla extract – 1 tsp.
- Chopped walnuts – .33 cups

Preparation Method:

1. Blend the cocoa powder, sweetener, cheese, and butter using a fork or mixer. Stir in the walnuts, coconut, salt, and vanilla extract.
2. Scoop out one-inch balls to make haystacks. Chill approximately 30 minutes or longer.

Peanut Butter & Chocolate Cups

Servings: 12

Macros: 2.2 g Net Carbs | 3.4 g Prot. | 26 g Fat | 246 Cal.

Ingredients:

- Coconut oil – 1 cup
- Heavy cream – 2 tbsp.
- Natural peanut butter or another butter – .5 cup
- Cocoa powder – 1 tbsp.
- Kosher salt – .25 tsp.
- Vanilla extract – .25 tsp.
- Roasted chopped salted peanuts or another nut – 1 oz.

Preparation Method:

1. Use the low setting on the stovetop to prepare a saucepan with the coconut oil. Once it's hot (3-5 min.), stir in the rest of the fixings.
2. Pour into the silicone muffin molds or use an ice tray. Sprinkle with the nuts and put them on a baking tray.
3. Freeze until it's firm for about one hour. Pop out of the molds and place in an airtight container to enjoy.

Pecan Turtle Truffles

Servings: 15

Macros: 1 g Net Carbs | 14 g Fat | 4 g Prot. | 142 Cal.

Ingredients:

- Swerve or your preference – .33 cup
- Melted butter – .5 cup
- Vanilla extract – .25 tsp.
- Caramel extract – .5 tsp.
- Vanilla protein powder -0- carbs – .33 cup
- Finely ground pecans – 1 cup
- Lindt or your choice – 85% chocolate – 4 squares
- Pecan halves – 15

Preparation Method:

1. Combine the sweetener, butter, vanilla extract, caramel extracts, finely ground pecans and protein powder in a mixing container.
2. Roll into 15 truffles and place on a sheet of parchment or waxed paper.
3. Melt the chocolate in a baggie in the microwave for one minute. Snip the corner and squeeze the chocolate over the prepared truffles.
4. Garnish each truffle with a pecan half. Chill and enjoy any time.

Raspberry Fudge

Servings: 12
Macros: 4.4 g Net Carbs | 2.6 g Prot. | 25.3 g Fat | 242 Cal.

Ingredients:

- Cream cheese – 16 oz.
- Butter – 1 cup
- White sugar substitute – .25 cup
- Unsweetened cocoa powder – 6 tbsp.
- Heavy cream – 2 tbsp.
- Raspberry extract – 1 tsp.
- Vanilla extract – 2 tsp.
- Chopped walnuts – .33 cup

Preparation Method:

1. Take the cream cheese and butter out of the fridge ahead of time until it reaches room temperature. Next, combine the cream cheese and butter in a large microwavable container using an electric mixer. When smooth, mix with the rest of the fixings until well incorporated.
2. Microwave using the high setting for 30 seconds. Blend with the mixer again until smooth.
3. Empty into the prepared pan (1-inch layer). Cover and chill for at least 2 hours in the fridge.
4. Slice into 12 portions. Serve and enjoy or store for a delicious treat later.

Slow Cooked Sugar-Free Fudge

Servings: 30

Macros: 2 g Net Carbs | 1 g Prot. | 5 g Fat | 65 Cal.

Ingredients:

- Sugar-free chocolate chips – 2.5 cups
- Coconut milk – .33 cup
- Salt – 1 pinch or so
- Pure vanilla extract – 1 tsp.
- Vanilla liquid stevia – optional – 2 tsp.
- Suggested: 3-4 quart-size

Preparation Method:

1. Mix all of the goodies in the cooker. Close the lid and cook for two hours on the low setting.
2. Take the lid off and unplug the unit. Don't stir for 30 minutes to one hour. Lastly, mix for five minutes until creamy smooth.
3. Line a one-quart dish with some parchment paper. Spread the fudge into the plate, and chill until firm.

Walnut Fudge

Servings: 12

Macros: 1.1 g Net Carbs | 1.8 g Prot. | 14.1 g Fat | 134 Cal.

Ingredients:

- Cream cheese – 4 oz.
- Butter – 1 stick (+) 1 tbsp.
- Granulated sweetener 2 tbsp. or to taste
- Vanilla – 1 tsp.
- Dark cocoa powder – 3 tbsp.
- Walnut pieces – .33 cup

Preparation Method:

1. Let the cream cheese and butter warm up to room temperature and combine. Mix well until the lumps are gone.
2. Stir in the sweetener, cocoa, and vanilla. Combine well and add the nuts.
3. Add to a lined plate and store in the fridge to set. Slice and enjoy.

White Chocolate Bark

Servings: 12

Macros: -0- g Net Carbs | -0- g Prot. | 2 g Fat | 40 Cal.

Ingredients:

- Cocoa butter – .25 cup
- Low-carb sweetener – .33 cup
- Vanilla powder – 1 tsp.
- Hemp seed powder – .5 tsp.
- Toasted pumpkin seeds – 1 tsp.
- Salt
- Coconut oil – for the bowl

Preparation Method:

1. Chop the cocoa butter into fine bits. Add water to a double boiler and add the pieces to melt using the medium heat setting. Stir in the rest of the fixings.
2. Lightly grease a bowl using a spritz of oil and add the mixture.
3. Let it cool and break into 12 portions.

White Chocolate Pecan Halves

Servings: 10

Macros: 1.4 g Net Carbs | 2 g Prot. | 8.9 g Fat | 123 Cal.

Ingredients:

- Pecan halves – 10 oz.
- Caramel sugar-free candies – 10
- Cocoa butter – 2 oz.
- Erythritol – 3 tbsp.
- Cinnamon – dash

Preparation Method:

1. Warm up the oven to 300°F.
2. Place a piece of the caramel candy on top of each of the pecan halves. Bake until they are slightly melted.
3. In a saucepan, combine the Erythritol, cocoa butter, and cinnamon until creamy. Spoon over each of the nuts and chill in the refrigerator for two hours.
4. When ready, just enjoy!

Delicious Fat Bombs

Allspice Almond Fat Bombs

Servings: 8

Macros: 2 g Net Carbs | 5 g Prot. | 22 g Fat | 214 Cal.

Ingredients:

- Heavy cream – 5 tbsp.
- Almond butter – 10 tbsp.
- Coconut oil – 4 tbsp.
- Allspice – .25 tsp.
- Cocoa powder – 2 tsp.
- Liquid stevia – 6 drops
- Chopped almonds – optional

Preparation Method:

1. Mix the top six ingredients, and add the almonds (if using). Transfer the bombs into a mold or other container.
2. Freeze for approximately two hours. Top with chopped almonds.
3. Remove and enjoy.

Almond Butter Fat Bombs

Servings: 8

Macros: 1.7 g Net Carbs | 1.5 g Prot. | 14.7 g Fat | 145 Cal.

Ingredients:

- Almond butter – 9.5 tbsp.
- Melted coconut oil – .75 cup
- Liquid stevia – .25 tsp. or to your taste
- Melted salted butter – 9 tbsp.
- Cocoa – 3 tbsp.

Preparation Method:

1. Combine all of the components listed until smooth.
2. Add the final product to 24 mini muffin molds or use silicone candy molds.
3. Freeze for a minimum of 30 minutes. Pop them out and enjoy.

Almond – Choco Fat Bombs

Servings: 24

Macros: -0- g Net Carbs | 0.5 g Prot. | 9.6 g Fat | 75 Cal.

Ingredients:

- Cocoa powder – unsweetened – 3 tbsp.
- Organic coconut oil – 1 cup
- Sweetener – 3-4 tbsp.
- Almond butter – 1 cup
- Optional: Splash almond extract

Preparation Method:

1. On the stovetop using medium heat, warm up a pan. Melt the coconut oil and almond butter. Blend in the sweetener of your choice with the cocoa powder.
2. Take the pan off of the heat to add the almond extract. Empty the contents into a silicone candy mold.
3. Refrigerate/freeze until set.
4. Store the goodies in an airtight container in the refrigerator.

Blackberry Coconut Fat Bombs

Servings: 16

Macros: 3 g Net Carbs | 1.1 g Prot. | 18.7 g Fat | 170 Cal.

Ingredients:

- Coconut butter – 1 cup
- Coconut oil – 1 cup
- Fresh or frozen blackberries – .5 cup
- Vanilla extract – .5 tsp.
- Stevia drops – add more for a sweeter taste
- Lemon juice – 1 tbsp.
- Also Needed: 6x6 container

Preparation Method:

1. Add the coconut oil, coconut butter, and frozen berries in a cooking pot using the medium heat setting. Line a baking pan with a sheet of parchment paper.
2. Use a small blender or food processor and add the mixture (step1) along with the rest of the components in the recipe. Spread it out on the prepared pan. Chill in the refrigerator for at least one hour.
3. *Note*: If you use fresh berries you won't need to cook them with the butter and coconut oil (step 1).

Blueberry Cream Cheese Fat Bombs

Servings: 12

Macros: 0.99 g Net Carbs | 0.96 g Prot. | 7.4 g Fat | 67 Cal.

Ingredients:

- Cream cheese – 1.5 cups
- Fresh or frozen berries – 1 cup
- Swerve – 2-3 tbsp.
- Vanilla extract – 1 tbsp.
- Coconut oil – .5 cup

Preparation Method:

1. For 30 to 60 minutes before preparation time, place the cream cheese on the countertop to become room temperature.
2. Take the stems off the berries and rinse. Pour into a blender. Mix well until smooth.
3. Pour in the Swerve and extract. Blend in the oil and cream cheese.
4. Add the mixture to candy molds and freeze for approximately two hours until set.

Bulletproof Fat Bombs

Servings: 20
Macros: 0.5 g Net Carbs | 0.8 g Prot. | 8.1 g Fat | 77 Cal.

Ingredients:

- Creamed coconut milk/full-fat cream cheese – 1 cup
- Butter – .25 cup
- Raw unsweetened cocoa powder – 2 tbsp.
- MCT oil/or more coconut oil – 2 tbsp.
- Swerve/Erythritol – .25 cup
- Liquid Stevia extract – 10-15 drops
- Strong brewed coffee – room-temperature – .5 cup
- Rum extract – optional – 1 tsp.

Preparation Method:

1. Combine the creamed milk and butter along with the cocoa powder, and stevia into a blender. Pulse until creamy smooth.
2. Pour in the coffee, pulse, and pour into an ice cream maker. Wait for approximately 30 to 60 minutes. The times will depend upon the type of maker used.
3. Empty the bombs into small muffin tins using about 2 tablespoons for each bomb. Let them cool for two to three hours in the freezer until firmed up.
4. *Note:* You can substitute 1-2 teaspoons of instant coffee powder and not need an ice-cream maker. You could also use a regular blender.

Cacao Coconut Fat Bombs

Servings: 12

Macros: 0.9 g Net Carbs | 0.7 g Prot. | 10.6 g Fat | 96 Cal.

Ingredients:

- Raw cacao powder – 1 tbsp.
- Liquid vanilla stevia – 5-10 drops
- Melted coconut oil – .5 cup
- Chopped almonds – optional – .25 cup
- Sea salt – a pinch – optional

Preparation Method:

1. Mix the cacao powder, stevia, and coconut oil.
2. Empty the mixture into parchment-lined muffin tins or a dish.
3. Put it in the fridge for at least one hour until firm. Pop the bombs out or cut into 12 portions.
4. Storage: Freezer for several months or the fridge for one week.

Chocolate Fat Bombs

Servings: 24

Macros: 1 g Net Carbs | 3 g Prot. | 21 g Fat | 180 Cal.

Ingredients:

- Coconut oil – .5 cup
- Splenda or your preference – 3 packets
- Walnut or almond butter – .25 cup
- Sugar-free coffee liqueur syrup – ex. Da Vinci – 2 tbsp.
- Heavy whipping cream – .25 cup
- Walnut halves – 24
- Also Needed: Silicon molds

Preparation Method:

1. Use a glass measuring cup and add the oil, walnut butter, coffee liqueur, cocoa powder, and sweetener.
2. Microwave 30-40 seconds. Stir the contents until the oil melts.
3. Stir in the cream and pour into the molds. Arrange a nut in each one and freeze until set.

Chocolate Peanut Butter Fat Bombs

Servings: 12

Macros: 1.1 Net Carbs | 1.7 g Prot. | 8.7 g Fat | 88 Cal.

Ingredients:

- Coconut oil – .25 cup
- Sugar-free peanut butter – .25 cup
- Unsweetened baking chocolate – 1 oz.
- Cocoa – 1 tbsp.
- Stevia drops – vanilla – .5 tsp.

Preparation Method:

1. Use a double boiler and melt the oil, peanut butter, cocoa, and baking chocolate.
2. Remove from the burner and add the stevia. Pour into the molds and freeze. When hard, store a closed plastic bowl in the freezer.

Chocolate Peppermint Fat Bombs

Servings: 6

Macros: 1.1 g Net Carbs | 0.4 g Prot. | 21 g Fat | 188 Cal.

Ingredients:

- Granulated sweetener – your choice – 1 tbsp.
- Melted coconut – 4.5 oz.
- Unsweetened coconut – 2 tbsp.
- Peppermint essence – .25 tsp.

Preparation Method:

1. Combine the sweetener, coconut oil, and peppermint essence.
2. Pour about half of the bomb into six ice cube trays. Let them stay in the fridge for a layer of white.
3. Use the remainder of the mixture to blend in with the cocoa powder.
4. Empty the chocolate mix on top of the trays.
5. Sit it back into the fridge until firm. Then, pop out and enjoy.

Coconut Macaroons Fat Bombs

Servings: 10

Macros: 0.5 g Net Carbs | 1.8 g Prot. | 5 g Fat | 46 Cal.

Ingredients:

- Shredded coconut – .5 cup
- Organic almond flour – .25 cup
- Swerve – 2 tbsp.
- Coconut oil – 1 tbsp.
- Vanilla extract – 1 tbsp.
- Egg whites – 3

Preparation Method:

1. In a mixing bowl, blend the swerve, coconut, and almond flour until well combined.
2. Warm the oil in a saucepan and stir in the vanilla.
3. Place a medium-sized bowl in the freezer.
4. Combine the oil into the flour mixture, mixing well.
5. Put the whites of the eggs into the cold dish and whisk until stiff – foamy peaks are formed. Fold in the whites with the flour.
6. Scoop the mixture into the baking sheet/muffin cups.
7. Bake until the macaroons are lightly browned or about eight minutes.
8. Cool before placing on a serving dish.

Coffee Fat Bombs

Servings: 15

Macros: -0- g Net Carbs | 4 g Fat | -0- g Prot. | 45 Cal.

Ingredients:

- Cream cheese – room temperature – 4.4 oz.
- Powdered Xylitol – 2 tbsp.
- Instant coffee – 1 tbsp.
- Coconut oil – 1 tbsp.
- Unsweetened cocoa powder – 1 tbsp.
- Room temperature butter – 1 tbsp.

Instructions:

1. Take the butter and cream cheese out of the fridge about an hour before it's time to begin.
2. With a blender/food processor, blitz the xylitol and coffee into a fine powder. Add the hot water to form a pasty mix.
3. Blend in the butter, cream cheese, cocoa powder, and coconut oil.
4. Add to ice cube trays and freeze a minimum of one to two hours.
5. Use Ziploc bags to keep them fresh in the freezer.

Coffee Fat Bombs

Servings: 15

Macros: -0- g Net Carbs | -0- g Prot. | 4 g Fat | 45 Cal.

Ingredients:

- Cream cheese – room temperature – 4.4 oz.
- Powdered xylitol – 2 tbsp.
- Instant coffee – 1 tbsp.
- Room temperature butter – 1 tbsp.
- Coconut oil – 1 tbsp.
- Unsweetened cocoa powder – 1 tbsp.

Preparation Method:

1. With a blender/food processor, blitz the xylitol and coffee into a fine powder. Add the hot water to form a pasty mix.
2. Blend in the butter, cream cheese, cocoa powder, and coconut oil.
3. Add to ice cube trays and freeze a minimum of one to two hours.
4. Use Ziploc bags to keep them fresh in the freezer.

Craving Buster Fat Bombs

Servings: 32

Macros: 2.25 g Net Carbs | 1.75 g Prot. | 22.5 g Fat | 122.5 Cal.

Ingredients:

- Organic cacao powder – 1 cup
- Melted organic coconut oil – 1 cup
- Almond butter – 1 cup
- Muffin tins – 32-count

Preparation Method:

1. Melt the oil and whisk in with the almond butter and cacao.
2. Spoon 1/2 tablespoon of the product into the 32 small paper muffin cups.
3. Freeze or refrigerate until hard and store in the fridge.
4. *Note:* If you want just one bomb; melt the oil and just add 1/2 tablespoon of each ingredient to enjoy.

Dark Chocolate Fat Bombs

Servings: 12

Macros: 5.6 g Net Carbs | 10.5 g Fat | 4 g Prot. | 96 Cal.

Ingredients:

- Stevia extract – 1 tsp.
- Butter/coconut oil – .5 cup
- Almond butter – .5 cup
- Dark chocolate – 85% or higher – 3 oz.
- Sea salt – .25 tsp.

Preparation Method:

1. With the use of a double boiler, combine all of the components in the recipe until smooth.
2. Empty the mixture into 12 ice trays and freeze for a minimum of one hour.
3. Serve or enjoy when the sugar urge strikes.

Dark Chocolate Raspberry Fat Bombs

Servings: 14

Macros: 2.6 g Net Carbs | 2.2 g Prot. | 17 g Fat | 164 Cal.

Ingredients:

- Extra-virgin coconut oil – 3 tbsp.
- Cocoa butter – .5 cup
- Unsweetened dark chocolate – 100% cacao – 4.2 oz.
- Unsweetened vanilla extract – 1 tsp. or 1 vanilla bean
- Unsweetened cacao powder – .33 cup
- Stevia extract – vanilla/clear/chocolate – 20-25 drops
- Swerve or Erythritol – powdered – 1/2 – 3/4 cup

Preparation Method:

1. Roast the almonds in a pan for five minutes.
2. Add an almond to each raspberry and freeze for one hour.
3. Using a dish over a pan of hot water or a double boiler, melt the unsweetened chocolate, coconut oil, and cocoa butter. Powder the Swerve for a smooth texture in a blender.
4. Remove the seeds from the bean (if using) by slicing the bean lengthwise and scraping out the seeds. Add them along with the unsweetened cacao, stevia, and powdered Erythritol.
5. Pour the mixture into papers with the use of a mini muffin tin, one tablespoon for each one. Add two loaded

raspberries and pour one more tablespoon of the chocolate to cover.

6. Put the bombs in the freezer until set, for about 30 minutes.

Lemonade Fat Bombs

Servings: 2

Macros: 7 g Net Carbs | 4 g Prot. | 43 g Fat | 404 Cal.

Ingredients:

- Cream cheese – 4 oz.
- Butter – 2 oz.
- Lemon zest & juice – .5 of 1 lemon
- Swerve – 2 tsp.
- Pink Himalayan salt – 1 pinch or to taste

Preparation Method:

1. Take the butter and cream cheese out of the fridge and let it become room temperature before using. Zest the lemon and juice it into a small dish.
2. In another container, mix the butter with the cream cheese. Use a hand mixer to combine all of the fixings until well mixed.
3. Spoon the mixture into small molds or cupcake paper liners in a muffin tin pan.
4. Stick the chosen holder in the freezer for two hours. Take them out of the molds and put them in a zipper-top baggie to enjoy any time. Store in the freezer for up to three months.

Maple Almond Fudge Fat Bombs

Servings: 24

Macros: 1.5 g Net Carbs | 1 g Prot. | 6 g Fat | 58 Cal.

Ingredients:

- Coconut oil – 2 tbsp.
- Butter – .25 cup
- All-natural almond butter – .5 cup
- Sugar-free maple syrup – 1 tbsp.
- Also Needed: Mini muffin tin & paper liners

Preparation Method:

1. Melt the butter, almond butter, and coconut oil for two minutes in the microwave. Stir every 30 seconds until melted. Whisk in the syrup and stir.
2. Pour the fixings into the prepared tins. Place in the fridge until hardened. Dice into 24 bite-sized pieces.
3. You can also store in the freezer or at room temperature, depending on the desired consistency.

Pistachio & Almond Fat Bombs

Servings: 36

Macros: 3.1 g Net Carbs | 2.2 g Prot. | 17.4 g Fat | 170 Cal.

Ingredients:

- Roasted almond butter – 1 cup
- Firm coconut oil – 1 cup
- Creamy coconut butter – 1 cup
- Cacao butter – melted – .5 cup
- Full-fat coconut milk – .5 cup
- Chai spice – 2 tsp.
- Ghee – .25 cup
- Pure vanilla extract – 1 tbsp.
- Raw shelled pistachios – .25 tsp.
- Himalayan salt – .25 tsp.
- Pure almond extract – .25 tsp.
- Also Needed: 9-inch square baking pan

Preparation Method:

1. Chill the coconut milk overnight.
2. Grease the pan and line it with parchment paper.
3. Melt the butter in a saucepan or microwave and set aside.
4. Add everything except the pistachios and cacao butter in a large bowl. Use the slow speeds and increase using a hand mixer until it is airy and light.

5. Empty the melted cacao into the almond mix and continue mixing until it is well incorporated.
6. Add it to the prepared pan and sprinkle with the chopped pistachios.
7. Refrigerate at least four hours. It is much better if chilled overnight.
8. Cut into 36 squares and enjoy.

Raspberry Coconut Bark Fat Bombs

Servings: 12

Macros: 2.45 g Net Carbs | 1.7 g Prot. | 23.6 g Fat | 234 Cal.

Ingredients:

- Powdered swerve sweetener – .25 cup
- Freeze-dried raspberries – .5 cup
- Coconut oil – .5 cup
- Coconut butter – .5 cup
- Unsweetened shredded coconut – .5 cup
- Also Needed: 8 x 8 pan with parchment paper

Preparation Method:

1. Prepare the baking pan and grind the berries in a food processor or coffee grinder until they are powdery.
2. Using the medium heat setting, add the oil, butter, sweetener, and coconut in a small saucepan. Stir until combined.
3. Pour half of the mixture into the pan and add the raspberry mixture to the other half of the batter and stir.
4. Drop by the spoonful into the coconut base and swirl to make a pretty design. Refrigerate or freeze and break into chunks for a tasty snack.

Stuffed Pecan Fat Bombs

Servings: 1

Macros: 2 g Net Carbs | 11 g Prot. | 31 g Fat | 150 Cal.

Ingredients:

- Pecan halves – 4
- Neufchatel cheese/cream cheese – 1 oz.
- Coconut butter/unsalted butter – .5 tbsp.
- Sea salt – 1 pinch
- Your favorite flavor mix – herb or veggie

Preparation Method:

1. Warm up the oven to 350°F oven. Once it's hot, toast the pecans for 8 to 10 minutes. Let cool.
2. Allow the cream cheese and butter to soften. Add the mixture with your favorite flavor, veggie, or herb and mix until smooth.
3. Spread the tasty fixings between the two pecan halves.
4. Drizzle with some sea salt.

Chapter 3: Cookies Galore

You are sure to find the perfect cookie for any time of the day or night!

Amaretti Cookies

Servings: 16

Macros: 1 g Net Carbs | 2.5 g Prot. | 8 g Fat | 86 Cal.

Ingredients:

- Coconut flour – 2 tbsp.
- Almond flour – 1 cup
- Baking powder – .5 tsp.
- Cinnamon – .25 tsp.
- Salt – .5 tsp
- Erythritol – .5 cup
- Eggs – 2
- Coconut oil – 4 tbsp.
- Vanilla extract – .5 tsp
- Almond extract – .5 tsp
- Sugar-free jam – 2 tbsp.
- Shredded coconut – 1 tbsp.

Preparation Method:

1. Line a baking tin with parchment paper. Warm up the oven to reach 400°F. Combine all of the dry fixings. After combined, work in the wet ones.
2. Shape into 16 cookies. Make a dent in the center of each one. Bake for 15-17 minutes.
3. Let them cool a few minutes before adding a dab of jam to each one and a sprinkle of the coconut bits.

Chocolate Cookies

Servings: 16
Macros: 10 g Net Carbs | 17 g Prot. | 14 g Fat | 155 Cal.

Ingredients:

- Butter – 7 tbsp.
- Almond flour – 2 cups
- Granulated sweetener – .75 cup
- Dark chocolate – 2 oz.
- Eggs – 2
- Orange zest – 1 tbsp.
- Orange extract – 1 tsp.
- Vanilla extract – 1 tsp.
- Orange juice – 1 tbsp.
- Baking powder – .75 tsp.
- Baking soda – .5 tsp.
- Salt – .5 tsp.

Preparation Method:

1. Warm up the oven to reach 350°F.
2. Combine the dry fixings (baking soda, salt, flour, baking powder, and sweetener).
3. Use a microwavable dish to melt the butter and stir in the orange zest, juice, the orange extract, and vanilla extract.
4. Combine all of the fixings and mix well.
5. Add the dough onto a baking tin. Form into a rectangle and slice into 16 servings. Bake for 20-25 minutes.

Chocolate Chip Cookies

Servings: 24

Macros: 2 g Net Carbs | 2 g Prot. | 8 g Fat | 90 Cal.

Ingredients:

- Molasses – optional – .5 tsp.
- Large egg – 1
- Sweetener – swerve – .66 cup
- Cold – room temperature butter – 5.5 tbsp.
- Vanilla extract – .5 tsp.
- Almond flour – 1.25 cups
- Sea salt – optional – .125 tsp.
- Baking powder – 1.5 tsp.
- Coconut flour – 1 tbsp.
- Chopped pecans – optional – .25 cup
- Chocolate chips – sugar-free – .5 cup

Preparation Method:

1. Use some parchment paper or silicone baking mats to line two baking sheets. Set the oven temperature to 325°F. Use a mixer to blend the sweetener and butter. Mix in the molasses, egg, and vanilla extract until well combined.
2. In another container, combine the two flours, sea salt, and baking powder, stirring until blended.

3. Fold in the pecans and chocolate chips. Arrange the cookie dough by the tablespoonful into the prepared pans. They should be 1.5-inches apart.

    Bake until the bottoms are browned or about 12-15 minutes. Let them cool until firm and set (minimum 25 minutes).

Chocolate Coconut Cookies

Servings: 20

Macros: 1 g Net Carbs | 2.2 g Prot. | 6.8 g Fat | 77 Cal.

Ingredients:

- Almond flour – 1 cup
- Coconut flour – 3 tbsp.
- Salt – .25 tsp.
- Unsweetened shredded coconut – .33 cup
- Erythritol – .33 cup
- Baking powder – .5 tsp.
- Cocoa powder – .25 cup
- Coconut oil – .25 cup
- Vanilla extract – .25 tsp.
- Room-temperature eggs – 2

Preparation Method:

1. Warm up the oven to 350°F. Cover a baking tin with some parchment paper.
2. Combine the dry fixings and mix with a hand mixer.
3. In another dish, combine the wet components and add to the dry until well blended.
4. Break apart pieces of the cookie dough and roll into 20 balls.
5. Arrange on the cookie sheet and bake 15-20 minutes.

Chocolate-Filled Peanut Butter Cookies

Servings: 20
Macros: 2.7 g Net Carbs | 4.5 g Prot. | 14 g Fat | 150 Cal.

Ingredients:

- Almond flour – 2.5 cups
- Peanut butter – .5 cup
- Coconut oil – .25 cup
- Erythritol – .25 cup
- Maple syrup – 3 tbsp.
- Vanilla extract – 1 tbsp.
- Baking powder – 1.5 tsp.
- Salt – .5 tsp
- Dark chocolate bars – 2-3

Preparation Method:

1. Prepare a baking tin with a sheet of parchment paper.
2. Warm up the oven to reach 350°F.
3. Whisk each of the wet fixings together. Mix each of the dry ingredients. Sift them into the wet components. Mix well and place in the fridge for 20-30 minutes.
4. Break the bars into small squares. Shape the dough into little balls and press until they are flat. Add 1-2 pieces of chocolate and seal into the ball.
5. Arrange on the cookie sheet and bake for about 15 minutes. Remove and enjoy!

Chocolate Macaroon Cookies with Coconut

Servings: 20

Macros: 1 g Net Carbs | 2.2 g Prot. | 7 g Fat | 77 Cal.

Ingredients:

- Almond flour – 1 cup
- Coconut flour – 3 tbsp.
- Cocoa powder – .25 cup
- Baking powder – .5 tsp.
- Erythritol – .33 cup
- Shredded unsweetened coconut – .33 cup
- Salt – .25 tsp.
- Room temperature eggs – 2
- Coconut oil – .25 cup
- Vanilla extract – 1 tsp.

Preparation Method:

1. Line a baking tin with some aluminum foil.
2. Warm up the oven to reach 350°F.
3. Sift all of the dry fixings into a mixing container. Slowly add the wet components, mixing well.
4. Roll the dough into small balls and place on the prepared pan – several inches apart.
5. Bake for 15 to 20 minutes.
6. Sprinkle with the shredded coconut and enjoy.

Coconut Almond Cookies

Servings: 6

Macros: 2 g Net Carbs | 7 g Prot. | 25 g Fat | 271 Cal.

Ingredients:

- Almond flour – 1.25 cups
- Unsweetened shredded coconut – .5 cup
- Large eggs – 3
- Softened butter – 6 tbsp.
- Sugar substitute – .33 cup
- Almond extract – 1 tsp.
- Ground cinnamon – .25 tsp.
- Sea salt – .25 tsp.

Preparation Method:

1. Warm up the oven to reach 350°F.
2. Spritz a baking tin with some cooking oil spray.
3. Combine the sweetener of choice and softened butter.
4. One at a time, whisk and stir in the eggs until well incorporated.
5. Stir in the rest of the fixings – with the coconut added last.
6. Drop by the spoonful onto the prepared baking sheet. Bake for 12 to 15 minutes. Cool on a wire rack before storing.

Coconut No-Bake Cookies

Servings: 20

Macros: -0- g Net Carbs | 3 g Prot. | 10 g Fat | 99 Cal.

Ingredients:

- Melted coconut oil – 1 cup
- Monk fruit sweetened maple syrup or your favorite – .5 cup
- Shredded unsweetened coconut flakes – 3 cups

Preparation Method:

1. Cut out a sheet of parchment paper and place on a cookie tray.
2. Combine all of the fixings.
3. Run your hands through some water from the tap and shape the mixture into small balls. Arrange them on the pan around one to two inches apart.
4. Press them down to form a cookie and refrigerate until firm.
5. You can prepare these into individual bags if you're an on-the-go kind of person. It will stay fresh covered for up to 7 days (room temperature). Store in the fridge for up to a month or frozen up to two months.

Cream Cheese Cookies

Servings: 75 – 4 each

Macros: 2 g Net Carbs | 4 g Prot. | 19 g Fat | 204 Cal.

Ingredients:

- Surkin:1 or your favorite sugar substitute – .75 cup
- Softened cream cheese – 4 oz.
- Butter – 1 cup
- Egg – 1
- Coconut flour – .5 cup
- Almond flour – 2 cups

Preparation Method:

1. Warm up the oven to 350°F.
2. Cream the sweetener and butter until fluffy. Fold in the cream cheese and add the egg. Stir in both flours and mix in the vanilla.
3. Chill the prepared dough for a minimum of four hours.
4. Squeeze the dough into a cookie press. You can also roll it into a log and slice.
5. Bake 8-10 minutes – pressed cookies or 10-12 minutes – sliced.

Ginger Snap Cookies

Servings: 1

Macros: 2.2 g Net Carbs | 2.25 g Prot. | 6.7 g Fat | 74 Cal.

Ingredients:

- Ground cloves – .25 tsp.
- Nutmeg – .25 tsp.
- Salt – .25 tsp.
- Almond flour – 2 cups
- Ground cinnamon – .5 tsp.
- Unsalted butter – .25 cup
- Vanilla extract – 1 tsp.
- Large egg – 1

Preparation Method:

1. Warm up the oven temperature to 350°F.
2. Whisk the dry components in a mixing bowl. Blend in the rest of the ingredients into the dry mixture using a hand blender. The dough will be stiff.
3. Measure out the dough for each cookie and flatten with a fork or your fingers.
4. Bake for about 9-11 minutes or until browned.

Nut Butter Cookies

Servings: 10

Macros: 7 g Net Carbs | 5 g Prot. | 22 g Fat | 235 Cal.

Ingredients:

- Almond butter – 8.8 oz.
- Powdered Erythritol – .25 cup
- Egg – 1
- Salted butter – .25 tsp.
- Raw coconut butter – .25 cup

Preparation Method:

1. Warm up the oven to 320°F. Prepare a cookie sheet with a sheet of parchment paper.
2. Using a double boiler, melt the almond butter. Take it from the heat and stir in the Erythritol, salt, and egg. Fold until well mixed.
3. Break into 10 segments and roll into balls. Place on the prepared pan and flatten with a fork or your hand.
4. Bake for 12 minutes until browned to your liking.

Orange Walnut Cookies

Servings: 10

Macros: 4 g Net Carbs | 7 g Prot. | 17 g Fat | 137 Cal.

Ingredients:

- Walnut halves – 8 oz.
- Minced orange – zested – 3 tbsp.
- Eggs – 1
- Stevia drops – 20
- Cinnamon – garnish
- Shredded coconut – garnish

Preparation Method:

1. Set the oven temperature to about 320°F. Toast the walnuts for about 10 minutes until browned. Add them to a food processor. Toss in the rest of the fixings and continue blending until it's smooth.
2. Shape into ten balls and slightly flatten. Drizzle with some shredded coconut.
3. Bake for 40 minutes. Cool on the rack a few minutes and add to a platter to finish cooling. Store in an air-tight container and enjoy any time.

P B & J Cookies

Servings: 6

Macros: 5 g Net Carbs | 18 g Fat | 9 g Prot. | 209 Cal.

Ingredients:

- Egg – 1
- Sugar substitute – stevia – .5 cup
- Creamy Keto-friendly peanut butter – .66 cup
- Sugar-free strawberry preserves – .33 cup
- Almond flour – .33 cup
- Sea salt – .25 tsp.
- Baking powder – .25 tsp.
- Pure vanilla extract – .25 tsp.

Preparation Method:

1. Warm up the oven to 350°F. Spray a cookie sheet with a spritz of cooking oil or a layer of parchment paper.
2. Whisk the egg and combine with the stevia and peanut butter. When it's creamy, add the flour, salt, baking powder, and vanilla.
3. Mix well and shape into small balls. Make an indention in each one and add 1 teaspoon of preserves.
4. Bake until browned (10-12 min.). Cool on a wire rack and serve.

Peanut Butter Cookies

Servings: 6

Macros: 2 g Net Carbs | 7 g Prot. | 14 g Fat | 160 Cal.

Ingredients:

- Almond butter/Natural peanut butter/ your favorite – .5 cup
- Coconut flour – .5 cup
- Sugar substitute/Maple syrup – .25 cup
- Egg – 1
- Pure vanilla extract – .25 tsp.
- Sea salt – 1 pinch

Preparation Method:

1. Warm up the oven until it reaches 350°F. Cut out a sheet of parchment paper to fit a metal baking tray or spritz with a misting of cooking oil spray.
2. Combine all of the fixings. Prepare using an electric mixer until a dough is formed. Shape into little balls for the cookies. Arrange on the baking tin. Use a fork and make a crisscross pattern on each one.
3. Bake until golden or about 14—16 minutes.

Strawberry Thumbprints

Servings: 16
Macros: 1 g Net Carbs | 2g Prot. | 9 g Fat | 95 Cal.

Ingredients:

- Almond flour – 1 cup
- Baking powder – .5 tsp.
- Coconut flour – 2 tbsp.
- Salt – .5 tsp.
- Cinnamon – .5 tsp.
- Sugar-free strawberry jam – 2 tbsp.
- Shredded coconut – 1 tbsp.
- Erythritol – .5 cup
- Whisked eggs – 2
- Coconut oil – 4 tbsp.
- Almond extract – .5 tsp.
- Vanilla extract – .5 tsp.

Preparation Method:

1. Set the oven temperature to 350°F. Cover a cookie tin with a sheet of parchment paper.
2. Whisk the dry fixings and make a hole in the middle. Combine and fold in the wet fixings to form a dough. Break it into 16 segments and roll into balls.
3. Arrange each one on the prepared cookie sheet and bake 15 minutes.
4. When done; cool completely, and add a dab of jam to each one with a sprinkle of coconut.

Chapter 4: Bar Cookies

You will find a tasty batch in one of these cookie bars.

Almond Pumpkin Seed Bars

Servings: 8

Macros: 3.8 g Net Carbs | 4.7 g Prot. | 25 g Fat | 261.5 Cal.

Ingredients:

- Almond flour – 1 cup
- Melted butter – divided – .25 cup
- Erythritol – divided – .25 cup
- Salt – .5 tsp.
- Almond butter – .25 cup
- Heavy cream – .25 cup
- Cinnamon – .5 tsp.
- Maple extract – 1 tsp.
- Xanthan gum – .25 tsp.
- Toasted pumpkin seeds – .5 cup
- Also Needed: 8 x 8-inch baking pan

Preparation Method:

1. Warm up the oven until it reaches 400°F. Prepare a baking pan with a layer of parchment paper.
2. Combine 1/4 cup of the butter, salt, almond flour, and 1 tablespoon of the Erythritol. Mix well.
3. Press the crust (above) into the baking pan or dish. Bake for 12 to 15 minutes. Transfer to the countertop and let it cool.
4. Use a blender to combine the almond butter, rest of the melted butter, xanthan gum, maple extract, cinnamon, and heavy cream. Blend until smooth and creamy. Scoop it into the prepared crust and top with the toasted pumpkin seeds.
5. Store in the fridge for a minimum of two hours— overnight is best.
6. Slice into 8 squares.

Cheesecake Mocha Bars

Servings: 16

Macros: 3.24 g Net Carbs | 6.1 g Prot. | 21.2 g Fat | 232 Cal.

Ingredients for the Brownie Layer:

- Vanilla extract – 2 tsp.
- Unsalted butter – 6 tbsp.
- Large eggs – 3
- Almond flour – 1.5 cups
- Hershey's Baking Cocoa or your favorite – .5 cup
- Erythritol – 1 cup
- Salt – .5 tsp.
- Instant coffee – .5 tbsp.
- Baking powder – 1 tsp.

Ingredients for the Cream Cheese Layer:

- Erythritol – .5 cup
- Large egg – 1
- Softened cream cheese – 1 lb.
- Vanilla extract – 1 tsp.
- Also Needed: 8x8-inch baking pan

Preparation Method:

1. Set the oven temperature to 350°F. Lightly grease or spray the pan.
2. Combine the wet fixings starting with the vanilla and butter. Next, mix in the eggs.

3. In another container, combine the dry ingredients and whisk with the wet fixings. Set aside 1/4 cup of the batter for later. Pour the mixture into the pan.

4. Mix the cream cheese (room temperature) with the rest of the ingredients for the second layer. Spread it on the sheet of brownies.

5. Use the reserved batter as the last layer (will be thin). Bake 30-35 minutes. When cooled, slice the cheesecake bars, and enjoy.

Chia Bars

Servings: 14

Macros: 1.5 g Net Carbs | 2.5 g Prot. | 11 g Fat | 121 Cal.

Ingredients:

- Toasted almonds – .5 cup
- Coconut oil – divided – 1 tbsp. (+) 1 tsp.
- Erythritol – 4 tbsp. – divided
- Butter – 2 tbsp.
- Heavy cream – .25 tsp.
- Liquid stevia – .25 tsp.
- Vanilla extract – 1.5 tsp.
- Unsweetened & shredded coconut flakes – .5 cup
- Chia seeds – .25 cup
- Coconut cream – .5 cup
- Coconut flour – 2 tbsp.
- Also Needed: Food Processor

Preparation Method:

1. Add the toasted almonds into the food processor and pulse until crumbly.
2. Toss in 1 tablespoon of the coconut oil and 2 tablespoons of the Erythritol. Continue processing until you have almond butter. (Now you have another new usable product.)

3. Warm up a pan and add the butter, heavy cream, Erythritol, stevia, and vanilla. Stir until they're bubbly and fold in the almond butter. Stir to blend.

4. In a blender, grind the chia seeds to make a powdery mix. In another pan, toast the coconut flakes and mix with the chia seeds. Melt the coconut cream in a separate skillet.

5. Now, combine all of the fixings and add the melted coconut cream, flour, and coconut oil. Store in the fridge for one hour.

6. When it's ready, slice into squares and store in the refrigerator.

Coconut Cashew Protein Bars – No-Bake

Servings: 12

Macros: 8.3 g Net Carbs | 11 g Prot. | 16 g Fat | 212 Cal.

Ingredients:

- Coconut butter – .5 cup
- Cashew butter – .25 cup
- Coconut oil – .25 cup
- Ground flaxseed – .66 cup
- Protein powder –your favorite – 1.33 cups
- Coconut or cashew milk – .25 cup
- Liquid stevia coconut drops – .5 tsp.
- Optional Topping: Unsweetened coconut flakes
- Also Needed: 8 x 8-inch baking dish

Preparation Method:

1. Soften the coconut butter, cashew butter, and coconut oil in the microwave or saucepan. Stir to incorporate and set aside to cool.
2. In another container, whisk the flaxseed and protein powder. Stir in the milk.
3. Taste test the cashew/coconut mixture for sweetness and adjust accordingly. Combine the rest of the fixings, mixing well.
4. Portion into 12 servings and enjoy.

Coconut Chia Bars

Servings: 6 bars

Macros: 3.5 g Net Carbs | 4 g Prot. | 14 g Fat | 164 Cal.

Ingredients

- Water – .5 cup
- Chia seeds – 4 tbsp.
- Coconut oil – 1 tbsp.
- Confectioners Swerve – 1 tbsp.
- Vanilla extract – .25 tsp.
- Shredded dried coconut meat – unsweetened – 1 cup
- Cashews – .5 cup
- Also Needed: 9 x 9 cookie sheet

Preparation Method:

1. Set the oven temperature to 350°F.
2. Soak the seeds 15 minutes until gel-like, and mix with the coconut, oil, swerve, and vanilla extract. Lastly, add the cashews.
3. Line the mixture, using parchment paper, onto the baking tin. Press until it is about a 3/4-inch thickness, and bake for 45 minutes.
4. Slice into six bars and enjoy!

Coconut Cream Brownies

Servings: 6

Macros: 2 g Net Carbs | 3 g Prot. | 17 g Fat | 175 Cal.

Ingredients:

- Raw unsweetened cocoa powder – .25 cup
- Coconut flour – .25 cup
- Sugar substitute – .5 cup
- Sea salt – 1 pinch
- Melted coconut butter – .75 cup
- Coconut cream – .33 cup
- Melted butter or coconut oil – 2 tbsp.
- Egg – 1
- Pure vanilla extract – 1 tsp.
- Baking soda – .25 tsp.
- Also Needed: 9 x 3-inch loaf pan

Preparation Method:

1. Lightly spritz the pan with cooking oil spray. Warm up the oven to 350°F.
2. Whisk the cocoa powder, coconut flour, sugar substitute, salt, and baking powder in a large mixing container.
3. Mix the coconut butter, butter, and coconut cream. Whisk in the vanilla and egg.

4. Fold in the dry components and mix well. Arrange in the loaf pan. Bake until a toothpick inserted in the center comes out clean or about 20 minutes.
5. Cool at room temperature. Slice into squares and enjoy.

Dark Chocolate Brownies

Servings: 16
Macros: 4 g Net Carbs | 8 g Fat | 3 g Prot. | 76 Cal.

Ingredients:

- Cream cheese – 6 tbsp.
- Eggs – 3
- Coconut oil – 3 tbsp.
- Cocoa powder – heaping 2 tbsp.
- Almond flour – .25 cup
- Coconut flour – .25 cup
- Baking soda – .25 tbsp.
- Truvia – 9 packets
- Almond milk – .5 cup
- Vanilla extract – 1 tsp.
- Salt – 1 pinch

Preparation Method:

1. Warm up the oven to 375°F.
2. Lightly spritz the baking tin with cooking oil spray.
3. Whisk the eggs, cream cheese, coconut oil, almond milk, and vanilla extract.
4. In a separate container mix the dry fixings (almond flour, cocoa powder, coconut flour, Truvia, baking soda, and a pinch of salt).
5. Combine everything and scoop into the cake pan. Bake for about half an hour and chill before serving.

Easy Brownie in a Mug

Servings: 1

Macros: 5 g Net Carbs | 35 g Prot. | 15 g Fat | 310 Cal.

Ingredients:

- Granulated sweetener – 1 tbsp.
- Eggs – 2
- Heavy cream – 1 tbsp.
- Protein powder – 1 scoop

Preparation Method:

- You will love this one. Just add the eggs, cream sweetener, and protein powder into the chosen mug. Mix well.
- Place the cup in the microwave for one minute. Remove with caution and enjoy.

Peanut Butter Protein Bars

Servings: 12 bars

Macros: 3 g Net Carbs | 7 g Prot. | 14 g Fat | 172 Cal.

Ingredients:

- Coconut or olive oil – for the pan
- Almond meal – 1.5 cups
- Chunky peanut butter – Keto-friendly – 1 cup
- Egg whites – 2
- Almonds – .5 cup
- Cashews – .5 cup
- Also Needed: Baking pan

Preparation Method:

1. Warm up the oven ahead of time until it reaches 350°F. Spritz a baking dish lightly with coconut or olive oil.
2. Combine all of the fixings and add to the prepared dish.
3. Bake 15 minutes and cut into 12 pieces once they're cooled.
4. Store in the fridge to keep them fresh.

Pumpkin Bars with Cream Cheese Frosting

Servings: 16

Macros: 2 g Net Carbs | 3 g Prot. | 13 g Fat | 139 Cal.

Ingredients:

- Large eggs – 2
- Coconut oil – .25 cup
- Pumpkin puree – 1 cup
- Cream cheese – 2 oz.
- Almond flour – 1 cup
- Vanilla extract – 1 tsp.
- Gluten-free baking powder – 2 tsp.
- Erythritol sweetener blend – .66 cups
- Pumpkin pie spice – 1 tsp.
- Sea salt – .5 tsp.

Ingredients for the Frosting:

- Powdered Erythritol – .5 cup
- Heavy cream – 1 tbsp. – optional
- Softened cream cheese – 6 oz.
- Vanilla extract – 1 tsp.
- Also Needed: 1 – 9 x 9 – baking pan

Preparation Method:

1. Warm up the oven until it reaches 350°F. Cover the baking pan with parchment paper.
2. In a double boiler or microwave, melt the coconut oil and cream cheese.
3. Combine the vanilla, eggs, cream cheese, and puree using a hand mixer until smooth (medium-speed).
4. Whisk the dry fixings (salt, pie spice, baking powder, sweetener, and flour).
5. Mix all the ingredients with the mixer until just combined and pour into the pan.
6. Bake for 20 to 30 minutes. Cool completely.
7. Prepare the frosting with each of the ingredients when the bars are cooled. If it's too thick, just add a little cream or milk.
8. Slice into 16 equal portions. Enjoy any time.

Tart Lemon-Lime Bars

Servings: 16

Macros: 2 g Net Carbs | 3.2 g Prot. | 19.2 g Fat | 192.3 Cal.

Ingredients:

- Almond flour – 1.5 cups
- Unsweetened shredded coconut for the crust – .5 cup
- Melted butter – divided – 1 cup
- Erythritol – .25 cup
- Freshly grated ginger – 1 tbsp.
- Lime – juice – .25 cup each
- Lime – zested – 1 tbsp.
- Lemon – juiced – .25 cup
- Egg yolks – 6
- Xanthan gum – .5 tsp.
- Plain gelatin – 2 tbsp.
- For the Garnish: Toasted shredded coconut – .25 cup
- Chopped fresh mint – 1 tbsp.

Preparation Method:

1. Cover an 8 x 8-inch pan with parchment paper. Warm up the oven to 350°F.
2. Mix the almond flour, ginger, Erythritol, 1/2 cup of the coconut, and 1/2 cup of melted butter. Press into the bottom of the baking dish. Bake until the crust is golden or for 10-12 minutes. Let it cool thoroughly.

3. Pour the rest of the butter into a pan using the low heat setting. Stir in the lime zest, lemon and lime juice.

4. Crack the eggs one by one. Separate and add the egg yolks. Continue to stir until thickened.

5. Transfer from the heat and add the gelatin and xanthan gum. Stir until it dissolves. Pour over the cooked crust. Return the pan to the hot oven and bake for 15-18 minutes. The bars should be set in the center.

6. Cool the bars slightly before you garnish with some fresh mint and toasted coconut.

7. Slice into bars and store or serve.

Chapter 5: Cakes & Cheesecakes

Cakes

Berries & Cream Keto Cake with Brown Sugar Whipped Cream

Servings: 1
Macros: 8 g Net Carbs | 16 g Prot. | 65 g Fat | 671 Cal.

Ingredients for the Cake Batter:

- Large eggs – 2
- Torani or your favorite Sugar-free vanilla bean sweetener syrup – .25 cup
- Melted ghee – not hot – 2 tbsp.
- Room temperature organic cream cheese – 2 tbsp.
- Almond flour – .25 cup
- Mixed berries – raspberries/blueberries/strawberries/etc. – .25 cup

Ingredients for the Whipped Cream:

- Heavy whipping cream – .25 cup
- Sugar-free brown sugar syrup – ex. Torani/your preference – .5 tbsp.

Preparation Method:

1. Toss the eggs, cream cheese, ghee, and sweetener in a single-serving blender. Scrape into a regular-size mug. Stir in the flour and berries. Place in the microwave for four minutes.
2. Rinse out the single-serve blender and add the cream and brown sugar sweetener. Puree until it stiffens – it's whipped cream.
3. Once the cake has finished baking, just let it cool for a minute and add the cream.

Chocolate Lava Cake

Servings: 4

Macros: 3 g Net Carbs | 8 g Prot. | 17 g Fat | 189 Cal.

Ingredients:

- Unsweetened cocoa powder – .5 cup
- Melted butter – .25 cup
- Eggs – 4
- Sugar-free chocolate sauce – .25 cup
- Sea salt – .5 tsp.
- Ground cinnamon – .5 tsp
- Pure vanilla extract – 1 tsp.
- Stevia – .25 cup
- Also Needed: Ice cube tray & 4 ramekins

Preparation Method:

1. Pour one tablespoon of the chocolate sauce into four of the tray slots and freeze.
2. Warm up the oven to 350°F. Lightly grease the ramekins with butter or a spritz of oil.
3. Mix the salt, cinnamon, cocoa powder, and stevia until combined. Whisk in the eggs – one at a time. Stir in the melted vanilla extract and butter.
4. Fill each of the ramekins halfway and add one of the frozen chocolates. Cover the rest of the container with the cake batter.

5. Bake for 13-14 minutes. When they're set, place on a wire rack to cool for about five minutes. Remove and put on a serving dish.
6. Enjoy by slicing its molten center.

Chocolate Roll Cake

Servings: 12

Macros: 3 g Net Carbs | 5 g Prot. | 25 g Fat | 275 Cal.

Ingredients for the Mix:

- Almond flour – 1 cup
- Melted butter – 4 tbsp.
- Eggs – 3
- Psyllium husk powder – .25 cup
- Cocoa powder – .25 cup
- Coconut milk – .25 cup
- Sour cream – .25 cup
- Erythritol – .25 cup
- Vanilla – 1 tsp
- Baking powder – 1 tsp.

Ingredients for the Filling:

- Cream cheese – 8 oz. pkg.
- Butter – 8 tbsp.
- Sour cream – .25 cup
- Erythritol – .25 cup
- Stevia – .25 tsp.
- Vanilla – 1 tsp.

Preparation Method:

1. Warm up the oven to 350°F.
2. Combine each of the dry fixings and combine slowly with the wet components.
3. Mix well and spread the dough over a foil-covered baking tin. Bake for 12 to 15 minutes. Transfer to the counter to cool slightly to handle.
4. Prepare the filling. Spread the mixture over the dough and roll up your cake. Be sure to make it tight and enjoy.

Gingerbread – Slow Cooker

Servings: 10

Macros: 8.6 g Net Carbs | 9.1 g | Prot. | 24.8 g Fat | 223 Cal.

Ingredients:

- Almond/sunflower seed flour – 2.25 cups
- Coconut flour – 2 tbsp.
- Salt – .25 tsp.
- Ground cloves – .5 tsp.
- Swerve sweetener – .75 cup
- Ground ginger – 1.5 tbsp.
- Dark cocoa powder – 1 tbsp.
- Ground cinnamon – .5 tsp.
- Baking powder – 2 tsp.
- Large eggs – 4
- Melted butter – .5 cup
- Water or almond milk – .66 cup
- Freshly squeezed lemon juice – 1 tbsp.
- Vanilla extract – 1 tsp.
- Recommended Size: 6-quarts

Preparation Method:

5. Spritz the cooker with some cooking oil spray.
6. Whisk the all of the flour, salt, cloves, baking powder, cinnamon, ginger, sweetener, and cocoa powder in a large mixing container.

7. Blend in the eggs, melted butter, almond milk or water, vanilla extract, and lemon juice.

8. Empty the batter into the slow cooker and cook until set – approximately
2.5 to 3 hours.

5. Garnish as desired and enjoy, but count those carbs.

Lemon Cake

Servings: 8

Macros: 5.2 g Net Carbs | 7.6g Prot. | 32.6 g Fat | 350 Cal.

Ingredients:

- Coconut flour – .5 cup
- Baking powder – 2 tsp.
- Almond flour – 1.5 cups
- Swerve (or) *Pyure* All-purpose – 3 tbsp.
- Xanthan gum – .5 tsp. optional
- Whipping cream – .5 cup
- Melted butter – .5 cup
- Zest & juice – 2 lemons
- Eggs – 2

Ingredients for the Topping:

- *Pyure* all-purpose/Swerve – 3 tbsp.
- Lemon Juice – 2 tbsp.
- Boiling water – .5 cup
- Melted butter – 2 tbsp.
- Recommended: 2-4-quart slow cooker

Preparation Method:

1. For the Cake: Mix the dry ingredients in a container. Whisk the egg, lemon juice and zest, butter, and whipping cream. Combine all of the fixings and mix well. Scoop out the dough into the prepared slow cooker.

2. For the Topping: Mix all of the topping ingredients in a container, and empty over the batter in the cooker.
3. Place the lid on the cooker for two to three hours on the high setting.
4. Serve warm with some fresh fruit or whipped cream.

Mocha Pudding Cake – Slow Cooker

Servings: 6
Macros: 3.76 g Net Carbs | 9.29 g Prot. | 29.8 g Fat | 413.5 Cal.

Ingredients:

- Coconut oil spray or butter – for the cooker
- Finely chopped unsweetened chocolate – 2 oz.
- Butter – large chunks – .75 cup
- Heavy cream – .5 cup
- Vanilla extract – 1 tsp.
- Instant coffee crystals – 2 tbsp.
- Almond flour – 1.33 cup
- Unsweetened cocoa powder – 4 tbsp.
- Salt – .125 tsp.
- Large eggs – 5
- Stevia Erythritol granulated sweetener – .66 cup
- Low-carb whipped cream/ice cream – Optional
- Recommended: 4-6-quart slow cooker

Preparation Method:

1. Grease the cooker with butter/spray.
2. Using the medium heat setting on the stovetop, melt the unsweetened chocolate and butter in a small pan. Whisk occasionally. Take it off of the burner and cool.
3. Whisk the heavy cream, vanilla extract, and coffee crystals in a small container.
4. Mix together the almond flour, cocoa, and salt in another dish.

5. Whip the eggs using a mixer (high-speed). Slowly add the sweetener when thickened. Beat on the high setting about five minutes.

6. Slowly, on the low setting, use the mixer to combine the unsweetened chocolate mixture and butter – adding it to the cake mixture.

7. Fold in the flour, salt, and cocoa mixture. Blend (medium speed), and add the coffee, cream, and vanilla ingredients.

8. Add the batter to the prepared slow cooker, and place a paper towel over the slow cooker top to absorb the moisture.

9. Secure the top and cook on low for 2.5 to 3.5 hours (4-quart cooker) or for 2-3 hours (6-quart cooker).

10. Test for doneness in the center at 160°F. The center will be a soft soufflé consistency with an outer cake-like appearance.

11. Enjoy, but remember to count the extra carbs.

Pumpkin Blondies

Servings: 12
Macros: 1.5 g Net Carbs | 2 g Prot. | 11 g Fat | 110 Cal.

Ingredients:

- Coconut oil – for the pan
- Egg – 1 large
- Softened butter – .5 cup
- Pumpkin puree – .5 cup
- Erythritol – .5 cup
- Almond flour – .25 cup
- Coconut flour – 2 tbsp.
- Cinnamon – 1 tsp.
- Pumpkin pie spice – .125 tsp.
- Liquid stevia – 15 drops
- Maple extract – 1 tsp.
- Chopped pecans – 1 oz.

Preparation Method:

1. Heat up the oven temperature to 350°F. Grease a baking pan with a spritz of coconut oil.
2. Using an electric mixer to blend the egg, butter, puree, and Erythritol.
3. Combine each of the flours with the pie spice, stevia, cinnamon, and maple extract.
4. Blend it all together and add to the awaiting tin. Sprinkle the top with pecans. Bake 20-25 minutes until the edges are lightly browned.

Raspberry Coconut Cake – Slow Cooker

Servings: 10
Macros: 6.7 g Net Carbs | 10.4 g Prot. | 32 g Fat | 362 Cal.

Ingredients:

- Unsweetened shredded coconut – 1 cup
- Almond flour – 2 cups
- Swerve sweetener – .75- 1 cup
- Large eggs – 4
- Powdered egg whites – .25 cup
- Salt – .25 tsp
- Baking soda – 2 tsp.
- Melted coconut oil – .5 cup
- Raspberries – fresh or frozen – 1 cup
- Coconut extract – 1 tsp.
- Almond or coconut milk – .75 cup
- Sugar-free dark chocolate chips – .33 cup
- Coconut oil or favorite cooking spray
- Recommended: 6-quart size

Preparation Method:

1. Spritz the inside of the slow cooker with some cooking oil spray.
2. Whisk the flour, sweetener, coconut, salt, baking soda, and powdered egg whites in a large mixing container.
3. Add the coconut or almond milk, eggs, coconut extract, and melted coconut oil. Stir well and fold in the chips and berries.
4. Spread the prepared batter into the cooker and cook on the low setting for three hours. Turn the unit off and let it cool.
5. Top with whipped cream and enjoy!

Raspberry Cream Cheese Coffee Cake – Slow Cooker

Servings: 12

Macros: 3.9 g Net Carbs | 7.5 g Prot. | 19.2 g Fat | 239 Cal.

Ingredients:

- Swerve sweetener – .5 cup
- Almond flour – 1.25 cups
- Salt – .25 tsp.
- Vanilla protein powder – .25 cup
- Coconut flour – .25 cup
- Baking powder – 1.5 tsp
- Large eggs – 3
- Water – .66 cup
- Organic butter – melted – 6 tbsp.
- Vanilla extract – .5 tsp.

Ingredients for the Filling:

- Powdered swerve sweetener – .33 cup
- Organic cream cheese – 8 oz.
- Large egg – 1
- Fresh raspberries – 1.5 cups
- Organic whipping cream – 2 tbsp.
- Suggested Size of Cooker: 6-quart

Preparation Method

1. Grease the insert of the cooker thoroughly and prepare the batter.
2. Combine the dry fixings. Stir in the melted butter, eggs,

and water.

3. Prepare the filling. Whip the sweetener and cream cheese until smooth. Whisk the whipping cream, vanilla extract, and egg until well mixed.

4. Assemble the cake using 2/3 of the batter into the prepared cooker.

5. Smooth the batter and add the cream cheese mixture. Sprinkle with the berries. Use a spoon to 'dot' the top of the cake mixture.

6. Prepare for three to four hours on the low setting or until the edges are browned. The filling may still have a little jiggle if shaken.

7. Turn off the cooker and remove the insert.

8. Let it cool before serving. It is also tasty served chilled.

Spice Cakes

Servings: 12
Macros: 3 g Net Carbs | 6 g Prot. | 27 g Fat | 277 Cal.

Ingredients:

- Salted butter – .5 cup
- Erythritol – .75 cup
- Eggs – 4 – divided
- Vanilla extract – 1 tsp.
- Ground clove – .25 tsp.
- Allspice – .5 tsp.
- Nutmeg – .5 tsp.
- Almond flour – 2 cups
- Baking powder – 2 tsp.
- Cinnamon – .5 tsp.
- Ginger – .5 tsp.
- Water – 5 tbsp.
- Also Needed: Cupcake tray

Preparation Method:

1. Heat up the oven temperature to 350°F. Prepare the baking tray with liners (12).
2. Mix the butter and Erythritol with a hand mixer. Once it's smooth, combine with 2 eggs and the vanilla. Add the rest of the eggs and mix well.
3. Grind the clove to a fine powder and add with the rest of the spices. Whisk into the mixture. Stir in the baking powder and almond flour. Blend in the water. When the batter is smooth; add to the prepared tin.
4. Bake for 15 minutes. Enjoy any time.

Strawberry & Cream Cakes

Servings: 5
Macros: 3.7 g Net Carbs | 30 g Fat | 6 g Prot. | 275 Cal.

Ingredients:

- Eggs – 3
- Cream cheese – 3 oz./6 tbsp.
- Baking powder – .25 tsp.
- Vanilla extract – .5 tsp.
- Erythritol – 2 tbsp.

Ingredients for the Filling:

- Strawberries – 10
- Heavy cream – 1 cup

Preparation Method:

1. Cover a baking sheet with parchment paper.
2. Break the eggs and which just the egg *whites*. Whisk to form stiff peaks.
3. In another dish; combine the cream cheese, egg *yolks*, vanilla extract, baking powder, and Erythritol.
4. Slowly add the egg mixtures together. Shape into cake forms and place on the lined baking tin.
5. Whip the heavy cream until thickened.
6. Bake for 25-30 minutes. Let them cool and add the berries and cream.

Zucchini Bread

Servings: 12

Macros: 13.8 g Net Carbs | 15.7 g Fat | 5 g Prot. | 174 Cal.

Ingredients:

- Almond flour – 1 cup
- Cinnamon – 2 tsp.
- Coconut flour – .33 cup
- Baking powder – 1.5 tsp.
- Optional: xanthan gum – .5 tsp
- Salt – .5 tsp.
- Baking soda – .5 tsp.
- Softened coconut oil or butter – .33 cup
- Eggs – 3
- Vanilla – 2 tsp.
- Pyure all-purpose – .5 cup
- Shredded zucchini
- Chopped pecans or walnuts – .5 cup
- Also Needed: 4x8 silicone bread pan

Preparation Method:

1. Combine the coconut and almond flour, salt, baking soda, and powder, cinnamon, and xanthan gum. Set aside for now.
2. Mix the oil, eggs, vanilla, and sugar in another dish. Combine the fixings.
3. Blend in the nuts and shredded zucchini. Scoop the batter into the prepared bread pan.

4. Arrange the cooker on the top rack (or on crunched up aluminum foil balls). You want it at least 1/2-inch from the bottom of the slow cooker.
5. Put the top on the cooker and prepare for three hours using the high-temperature setting.
6. Cool, wrap in foil, and place in the fridge. It is best when refrigerated.

Cheesecakes

Banana Split Cheesecake – No-Bake

Servings: 20

Macros: 6.7 g Net Carbs | 4.1 g Prot. | 30 g Fat | 302 Cal.

Ingredients for the Crust:

- Cinnamon – 2 tsp.
- Almond flour – 3 cups
- Swerve – .33 cup
- Melted butter – 1 cup

Ingredients for the Filling:

- Swerve confectioner's sugar – 1 cup
- Melted butter – 1 cup
- Cream cheese – 16 oz.

Ingredients for the Topping:

- Chopped banana – 1
- Sliced strawberries – 2 pints
- Lemon juice – 1 tbsp.
- Heavy whipping cream – 2 cups
- Gelatin – 1.5 tsp.
- Vanilla extract – 1 tsp.
- Swerve – 3 tbsp.
- Nuts – optional
- Water – 3 tbsp.
- Chocolate sauce – optional
- Also Needed: 9 x 13-inch pan

Preparation Method:

1. Combine the crust fixings and press together in the pan.
2. Mix the sweetener, melted butter, and cream cheese until creamy. Spread on top of the crust.
3. Combine the banana and strawberries in a mixing dish along with the lemon juice. Make the next layer.
4. Prepare the Topping: Combine the whipping cream and gelatin in the water and beat well. Blend in the vanilla extract and sweetener. Whip until it is creamy to cover and make the next layer.
5. Top with the chocolate sauce and nuts if you like it that way.

Cheesecake Cupcakes

Servings: 12

Macros: 2.1 g Net Carbs | 4.9 g Prot. | 20 g Fat | 204 Cal.

Ingredients:

- Butter – .25 cup – melted
- Almond meal – .5 cup
- Eggs – 2
- Softened cream cheese – 16 oz. pkg.
- Stevia or your favorite sweetener – .75 cup
- Vanilla extract – 1 tsp.

Preparation Method:

1. Warm up the oven until it reaches 350°F. Prepare a muffin tin with 12 paper liners.
2. Combine the butter and almond meal. Spoon into the cups to make a flat crust.
3. Whisk the vanilla, sweetener of choice, eggs, and cream cheese with an electric mixer until creamy. Scoop it in on top of the crust. Bake for 15-17 minutes.
4. Once they're done the cooking cycle, just remove and cool at room temperature. Store overnight or at least 8 hours.
5. Enjoy anytime for a delicious treat.

Individual Strawberry Cheesecakes

Servings: 4

Macros: 9 g Net Carbs | 8 g Prot. | 47 g Fat | 489 Cal.

Ingredients for the Crust:

- Almond flour – .5 cup
- Melted butter/coconut oil – 3 tbsp.
- Sugar substitute – your preference – .25 cup or Maple syrup

Ingredients for the Filling:

- Sugar substitute – 3 tbsp. or use Grade B maple syrup
- Strawberries – 6
- Cream cheese – 8 oz.
- Sour cream – .33 cup
- Pure vanilla extract – .5 tsp.

Ingredients for the Garnish:

- Strawberries – 4
- Fresh mint leaves

Preparation Method:

1. Combine the crust fixings in a mixing bowl. Blend well and divide into four small ramekins. Gently press with your fingers.
2. Prepare the filling in a food processor. Pulse until creamy smooth.
3. Divide it over the crust of each one and chill for an hour or until it's set.
4. Garnish with another berry if desired and serve. (Add the carbs for any added garnishes)

Lemon Mousse Cheesecake

Servings: 1

Macros: 1.7 g Net Carbs | 3.7 g Prot. | 30 g Fat | 277 Cal.

Ingredients:

- Lemon juice – 2 lemons approx. – .25 cup
- Cream cheese – 8 oz.
- Salt – .125 tsp.
- Lemon liquid Stevia – 1 tsp. or to your liking
- Heavy cream – 1 cup

Preparation Method:

1. Use a mixer to blend the lemon juice and cream cheese until it's creamy smooth. Add the remainder of the ingredients and whip until blended.
2. Taste test. Add to a serving dish and sprinkle with some lemon zest.
3. Refrigerate until you are ready to enjoy.

New York Cheesecake Cupcakes

Servings: 12

Macros: 14.7 g Net Carbs | 6.5g Prot. | 26.7 g Fat | 273 Cal.

Ingredients:

- Melted butter – 5 tbsp.
- Almond meal – .66 cup
- Cream cheese – 16 oz.
- Sour cream – .5 cup
- Swerve or another favorite – .75 cup
- Water – 2 tbsp.
- Heavy whipping cream – .25 cup
- Eggs -3
- Almond flour – 2 tbsp.
- Vanilla extract – 1.5 tsp.

Preparation Method:

1. Heat up the oven to reach 350°F. Prepare a 12-count muffin pan with paper liners.
2. Combine the butter and almond meal and spoon into the liners to form the crust.
3. Stir the sweetener and cream cheese until creamy. Blend in with the water and whipping cream. One at a time, add the eggs, stirring with each one.
4. Next, fold in the flour, sour cream, and extract. Spoon into the liners.

5. Bake for 15-18 minutes. Don't over-cook. The middle will be set when it's done. Cool on the countertop until room temperature. Then, store in the fridge overnight or a minimum of 8 hours.

Plain Cheesecake – No Bake

Servings: 6
Macros: 5 g Net Carbs | 6.9 g Prot. | 25 g Fat | 247 Cal.

Ingredients for the Crust:

- Melted coconut oil – 2 tbsp.
- Almond flour – 2 tbsp.
- Swerve Confectioner's/equivalent – 2 tbsp.
- Crushed salted almonds – 2 tbsp.

Filling Ingredients:

- Swerve confectioner's/equivalent – .25 cup
- Gelatin – 1 tsp.
- Cream cheese – 16 oz. pkg.
- Unsweetened almond milk – .5 cup
- Vanilla extract – 1 tsp.

Preparation Method:

1. Prepare the crust by combining all of the fixings under the crust section. Place one heaping tablespoon into the bottom of dessert cups. Press the mixture down and set aside.
2. Prepare the filling. Mix the sweetener and gelatin. Pour in the milk and stir (5 min.). Whip the vanilla beans and cream cheese with a mixer on medium until creamy. Add the gelatin mixture slowly until well incorporated.
3. Pour the mixture over the crust of each cup. Chill for three hours, minimum.

Chapter 6: Delicious Scones – Pies & Tarts

Pies & Scones

Blueberry Cream Pie

Servings: 16

Macros: 3 g Net Carbs | 5.4 g Prot. | 30 g Fat | 305 Cal.

Ingredients:

- Unsweetened shredded coconut – 1 cup
- Unsalted sunflower seeds – 1 cup
- Salt – .25 tsp.
- Softened butter – .25 cup

Filling Ingredients:

- Fresh or frozen blueberries – 1 cup
- Gelatin – 2.5 tsp/1 envelope
- Lemon juice – 2 tbsp.
- Water – 2 tbsp.
- Swerve sweetener – .75 tsp.
- Softened cream cheese – 16 oz.
- Liquid stevia – .5 tsp.
- Heavy cream – divided – 2 cups

Topping Ingredients:

- Heavy cream – 1 cup
- Blueberry mixture – reserved from the filling – .25 cup
- Vanilla liquid stevia – .5 tsp.
- Also Needed: 8 x 8 baking dish

Preparation Method:

1. Add all of the crust fixings in a food processor and pulse until combined. Coat the baking dish with a little non-stick cooking spray or a spritz of oil. Add the crust.
2. Process the lemon juice and berries in the food processor until chopped.
3. Pour the water into a pan. Once it starts boiling, add the gelatin, stir, and set aside to cool.
4. In a stand mixer, add the cream cheese, 3/4 cup of the berries, lemon stevia, and swerve – mixing until smooth. Stir in 1 cup of the heavy cream and blend two to three minutes. Drizzle with the gelatin and mix. Pour into the crust.
5. Add the other cup of heavy cream along with the rest of the berries and blend on the high setting in the mixture to form the topping.
6. Decorate the pie with the filling and chill in the fridge for two or three hours (overnight is best).
7. When ready to eat, decorate with a few berries.

Blueberry Scones

Servings: 12

Macros: 4 g Net Carbs | 2 g Prot. | 8 g Fat | 133 Cal.

Ingredients:

- Baking powder – 2 tsp.
- Almond flour – 1.5 cups
- Stevia – .5 cup
- Vanilla – 2 tsp.
- Raspberries – .75 cup
- Eggs – 3

Preparation Method:

1. Warm up the oven to 375°F. Prepare a baking pan with a piece of parchment paper.
2. Whisk the baking powder, flour, stevia, and vanilla. Whisk the egg and add it to the mixture. Fold in the raspberries.
3. Add the batter to the prepared baking sheet and place in the oven.
4. Bake 15 minutes and remove the scones from the oven.
5. Cool slightly before serving.

Creamy Lime Pie

Servings: 8

Macros: 4.2 g Net Carbs | 7 g Prot. | 38.6 g Fat | 386 Cal.

Ingredients:

- Almond flour – 1.5 cups
- Erythritol – divided – .5 cup
- Salt – .5 tsp
- Melted butter – .25 cup
- Heavy cream – 1 cup
- Egg yolks – 4
- Freshly squeezed key lime juice – .33 cup
- Lime zest – 1 tbsp.
- Cubed cold butter – .25 cup
- Vanilla extract – 1 tsp.
- Xanthan gum – .25 tsp.
- Sour cream – 1 cup
- Cream cheese – .5 cup

Preparation Method:

1. Warm up the oven to 350°F. Melt the butter in a pan.
2. Mix the salt, half or 1/4 cup of the Erythritol, and the almond flour. Slowly add the butter. Blend and press into a pie platter.
3. Bake in the preheated oven for 15 minutes. Remove when it's lightly browned. Let it cool.
4. In another saucepan, combine the egg yolks, heavy cream, rest of the Erythritol, lime zest and juice. Simmer

over medium heat for 7 to 10 minutes or until it starts to thicken.

5. Take the pan from the heat and add the xanthan gum, vanilla extract, cold butter, cream cheese, and sour cream. Whisk until smooth.

6. Scoop into the cooled pie shell. Cover and place in the fridge for four hours. For best results, leave it overnight.

Pumpkin Cheesecake Pie

Servings: 8

Macros: 6 g Net Carbs | 10 g Prot. | 44 g Fat | 460 Cal.

Ingredients:

- Almond flour – 1.75 cups
- Cinnamon – .5 tsp.
- Swerve – 3 tbsp.
- Melted butter – 1 stick

Ingredients for the Filling:

- Swerve – .66 cup
- Pumpkin puree – .66 cup
- Vanilla extract – .5 tsp.
- Cinnamon – .5 tsp.
- Allspice – .125 tsp.
- Nutmeg – .25 tsp.
- Large eggs – room temperature – 2
- Room-temperature – cream cheese – 16 oz.
- Also Needed: 9-inch pie plate

Preparation Method:

1. For the Crust: Combine the sweetener, cinnamon, and almond flour in the baking dish. Melt and stir in the butter. Press the fixings together.
2. For the Filling: Mix the sweetener, vanilla, and cream

cheese with an electric mixer. When smooth blend in the eggs, pumpkin, nutmeg, cinnamon, and allspice.

3. Scrape the filling into the prepared crust. Bake 35-40 minutes.

4. Remove when the filling is firm. Set aside to cool down on a wire rack.

5. Chill overnight or at least a few hours before serving in equal portions.

Tarts

Cheesecake Tarts

Servings: 12

Macros: 2.8 g Net Carbs | 9 g Prot. | 16 g Fat | 175 Cal.

Ingredients for the Crust:

- Melted butter – 3 tbsp.
- Almond flour – .75 cup

Ingredients for the Filling:

- Room temperature cream cheese – 12 oz.
- Egg – 1
- Erythritol – .25 cup
- Fresh lemon juice – 1 tbsp.
- Vanilla extract – 1 tsp.
- Salt – .25 tsp.

Ingredients for the Toppings:

- Sugar-free strawberry jam – .25 cup
- Blueberries – .25 cup

Preparation Method:

1. Warm up the oven temperature to reach 350°F. Cover a cupcake tin with paper or silicone cupcake liners.
2. Melt the butter and mix with almond flour. Stir well until it becomes crumbly.
3. Press the crust mixture into each liner. Bake until they are golden brown (5 to 8 min.).
4. Prepare the filling. Combine the cream cheese with a hand mixer until softened. Whisk the egg and add to the mixture with 1/4 cup of Erythritol sweetener. Next, add 1 teaspoon of vanilla extract, 1 tablespoon of fresh lemon juice and 1/4 teaspoon of salt and mix one last time.
5. Scoop out the filling into the baked crusts and bake for about 20 minutes.
6. Let them cool on the counter for about ten minutes. Garnish each one with a tsp. of the jam. Add a portion of fresh fruit over that. Try three to four berries for each mini cake.

Dark Chocolate Tart

Servings: 4

Macros: 6 g Net Carbs | 13 g Prot. | 46 g Fat | 490 Cal.

Ingredients for the Crust:

- Coconut flour – 1 cup
- Flaxseed meal – .25 cup
- Sugar substitute – your preference – 3 tbsp. or to taste
- Butter – .5 cup
- Egg whites – 4

Ingredients for the Filling:

- Raw unsweetened cocoa powder – .5 cup
- Heavy cream – 1 cup
- Gelatin powder – 2.5 tsp.
- Sugar substitute – .25 cup or to taste
- Pure vanilla extract – 1 tsp.
- Sliced pistachios – .25 cup

Preparation Method:

1. Warm up the oven to 375°F. Prepare a pie pan or small tart pan with a spritz of cooking spray.

2. Combine the crust fixings in a food processor. Pulse until well mixed. Press into the prepared pan/pans. Bake for 15 minutes.

3. When it is ready, put the pan on a rack to cool.

4. Prepare the filling by combining all of the components except for the pistachios into a blender. Mix well until creamy smooth.

5. Add the mixture to the prepared crust/crusts. Cover the pie with a sheet of plastic wrap. Place it in the fridge for about 2 hours. It should be firm.

6. When ready to serve, just add the sliced pistachios and enjoy.

Lemon Custard Tarts

Servings: 2

Macros: 2 g Net Carbs | 17 g Prot. | 95 g Fat | 954 Cal.

Ingredients for the Crust:

- Unsalted melted butter – 3 tbsp.
- Almond meal – .75 cup
- Optional: Dried lavender flowers – .5 tsp.
- Sugar-free Vanilla bean sweetener syrup – ex. Torani – 1 tbsp.

Ingredients for the Filling:

- Freshly squeezed lemon juice – .5 cup
- Large egg yolks – 4
- Grated zest of lemon – 3
- Unsalted butter – melted – .5 cup.
- Sugar-free vanilla syrup- your brand preference – .25 – .5 cup
- Also Needed: 2 crème Brule dishes – 4.5-inch x 1.25 thick

Preparation Method:

1. Heat up the oven to 375°F. Lightly spritz the dishes with some ghee or butter.

2. Prepare the Crust: If you're using the flowers, grind them into a fine dust with a mortar and pestle. Combine with the 3 tablespoons of melted butter and almond flour. Press into the bottom of the two dishes.

3. Bake until the tops start browning (10 min.). Transfer to the counter to cool.

4. Make the Filling: Use a food processor or blender to mix the lemon juice, sweetener, egg yolks, lemon zest and rest of the butter. Scoop into a saucepan (med-low) and simmer about 15 minutes or until it's pudding-like.

5. When ready, pour the filling over the two crusts. Secure a layer of plastic wrap over each one and refrigerate overnight.

Mini Chocolate Avocado Tarts

Servings: 4

Macros: 5 g Net Carbs | 11 g Prot. | 33 g Fat | 367 Cal.

Ingredients:

- Almond flour – 2 tbsp.
- Stevia or your choice – 1 tbsp.
- Large egg white – 1
- Flax meal – .25 cup
- Natural peanut butter/almond butter – 4 tbsp.
- Butter/coconut oil – 2 tbsp.
- Also Needed: 4 small tart tins

Ingredients for the Top Layer:

- Medium avocado – 1
- Unsweetened cocoa powder – 4 tbsp.
- Stevia sugar substitute – .25 cup.
- Heavy cream – 2 tbsp.
- Pure vanilla extract – .5 tsp.

Preparation Method:

1. Heat up the oven to reach 350°F.
2. Combine 1 tablespoon of the stevia, flax meal, almond flour, and egg white.

3. Press the crust into the tins. Bake for until they're golden brown or about 8 minutes. Transfer to the countertop and cool.
4. Melt the butter and peanut butter in a small saucepan (med-low heat). Stir well and divide into each of the shells. Chill for 30 minutes.
5. Mix the cocoa powder, avocado, stevia, vanilla extract, and heavy cream in a food processor or blender.
6. Take the tarts out of the fridge and garnish with the blended avocado mixture. Place it back in the refrigerator for an hour for a minimum of one hour. Serve.

Pumpkin Pecan Tarts

Servings: 2

Macros: 9 g Net Carbs | 19 g Prot. | 45 g Fat | 530 Cal.

Ingredients for the Crust:

- Almond flour – .5 cup
- Butter – melted – 2 tbsp.
- Cinnamon – 1 tsp.
- Salt – 1 pinch

Ingredients for the Filling:

- Ricotta cheese – .5 cup
- Pumpkin puree – .5 cup
- Pumpkin pie spice – .25 tsp.
- Cinnamon – 1 tsp.
- Vanilla extract – .5 tsp.
- Salt – A pinch
- So Nourished Erythritol – 2 tbsp.
- Whole egg – 1 (+) Egg white – 1

Ingredients for the Topping:

- Pecans – 16
- Sugar-free maple syrup

Preparation Method:

1. Heat up the oven to 350°F.
2. Combine the crust fixings in a mixing container. Mix well and press into mini tartlet pans (4.5-inch pans). Bake for about 10 minutes and set aside to cool.
3. Prepare the Filling: Combine all of the fixings. Pour into the cooled shells. Bake for 20 minutes (on a baking tin).
4. Remove and add some pecans to the tops. Place them back in the oven for 10 more minutes. The tops may be a little jiggly – but set.
5. Let them cool slightly and drizzle with the syrup of choice and a portion of whipped cream.

Chapter 7: Frozen Desserts

Ice cream never tasted so good—and they're Ketogenic!

Blueberry No-Churn Ice Cream

Servings: 4
Macros: 3 g Net Carbs | 2 g Prot. | 15 g Fat | 153 Cal.

Ingredients:

- Heavy whipping cream – 1 cup
- Fresh blueberries – .25 cup
- Sour cream or Crème Fraiche – .25 cup
- Beaten egg yolk – 1
- Pure vanilla extract – 2 tsp.

Preparation Method:

1. Use a hand mixer to whip the Crème Fraiche.
2. In another bowl, whip the heavy cream to form stiff peaks.
3. Carefully, fold them together. Puree the berries in a blender or food processor until smooth and creamy.
4. Combine the egg, with the puree, and vanilla. Combine all of the fixings until just combined.
5. Add to a loaf pan and freeze for 2 hours. Stir about every 30 minutes.
6. Enjoy anytime!

Butter Pecan Ice Cream

Servings: 4

Macros: 1 g Net Carbs | 3 g Prot. | 24 g Fat | 230 Cal.

Ingredients:

- Chopped pecans – .5 cup
- Xanthan gum – .125 tsp.
- Egg yolks – 2
- Pure vanilla extract – 1 tsp.
- Sugar substitute – .25 cup
- Butter- 2 tbsp.
- Heavy cream – 1 cup

Preparation Method:

1. Use the medium heat setting to melt the butter in a saucepan. Whisk in the cream. Stir in the sugar substitute and xanthan gum. Whisk well until combined and pour into a metal container to cool.
2. Next, slowly add the eggs using a hand mixer. Fold in the pecans and vanilla.
3. Place the container in the freezer for at least four hours – stirring every hour or so.
4. Remove from the freezer and serve with a few chopped pecans for the topping.

Chocolate Ice Cream

Servings: 4
Macros: 4.75 g Net Carbs | 1.75 g Prot. | 22.5 g Fat | 231 Cal.

Ingredients:

- Heavy whipping cream – 1 cup
- Powdered swerve/Erythritol confectioners – .33 cup
- Unsweetened cocoa powder – 1.5 tbsp.
- Vanilla extract – .5 tsp.
- Large egg yolks – 2

Preparation Method:

1. Warm up a saucepan using the medium-high heat setting. Stir in the whipping cream and swerve. Once it starts to boil; lower the heat setting to simmer.
2. Stir in the cocoa powder and mix well. Remove most of the chunks.
3. In another container, whisk the egg yolks and vanilla. Set to the side.
4. Once the mixture (step 1) has thickened, remove it from the burner to cool for about five minutes. Slowly combine the cream mixture to the yolks. Whisk with a hand mixer or a fork until it forms a frothy top.
5. Place in the freezer for 4-6 hours. Check several times. If it freezes overnight, you may want to let it sit out for a few minutes to be easier to scoop out of the container.

Chocolate Shakes

Servings: 2

Macros: 7 g Net Carbs | 4 g Prot. | 47 g Fat | 210 Cal.

Ingredients:

- Coconut milk – 4 oz.
- Heavy whipping cream – .75 cup
- Natural sweetener – swerve – 1 tbsp.
- Vanilla extract – .25 tsp.
- Unsweetened cocoa powder – 2 tbsp.

Preparation Method:

1. Empty the cream into a cold metal bowl. Use your hand mixer and cold beaters to form peaks.
2. Slowly add the milk into the cream. Add the rest of the fixings.
3. Stir well and portion into two glasses. Chill in the freezer one hour before serving. Tip: Stir a couple of times if possible.

Mint Chocolate Chip Shake

Servings: 2

Macros: 11 g Net Carbs | 4 g Prot. | 21 g Fat | 274 Cal.

Ingredients:

- Full-fat coconut milk – 1 cup
- Unsweetened dark chocolate – diced – 2 tbsp.
- Mint leaves – .5 cup
- Pitted avocado – .5 of 1
- Pure vanilla extract – 1 tsp.
- Sugar substitute or maple syrup – 1 tbsp.
- Ice – .5 cup

Preparation Method:

1. Combine each of the fixings in a high-speed blender (such as a NutriBullet). Pulse until smooth.
2. Serve immediately.
3. Tip: Add more ice if you like a thicker shake.

Peanut Butter Caramel Milkshake

Servings: 1

Macros: 5 g Net Carbs | 8 g Prot. | 35 g Fat | 365 Cal.

Ingredients:

- Coconut milk – 1 cup
- Ice cubes – 7
- Sugar-free salted caramel syrup – 2 tbsp.
- Natural peanut butter – 2 tbsp.
- MCT Oil – 1 tbsp.
- Xanthan gum – .25 tsp.

Preparation Method:

1. Combine each of the ingredients in a blender.
2. Mix well and serve in a chilled glass.

Pudding Pops

Servings: 1

Macros: 1.2 g Net Carbs | 2.8 g Prot. | 10.3 g Fat | 122 Cal.

Ingredients:

- Gelatin – 1 tsp.
- Vanilla extract – 1 tsp.
- Coconut/almond milk – from a carton – 1 cup
- Cocoa powder – 2 tbsp.
- Cream cheese – 6 oz.
- Liquid stevia – 20 drops
- Erythritol – powder – 1 tbsp.

Preparation Method:

1. Prepare a saucepan over low heat and add the milk. Mix in the gelatin slowly to dissolve. Remove from the burner when it starts steaming. Pour into a spouted container such as a measuring cup.
2. Combine the remainder of the fixings and use a blender to mix well.
3. Pour into a popsicle mold. Freeze for two hours – minimum.
4. Enjoy whenever that sweet urge strikes.

Pumpkin Ice Cream

Servings: 2

Macros: 3 g Net Carbs | 8 g Prot. | 20 g Fat | 250 Cal.

Ingredients:

- Butter – 1 tbsp.
- Chopped pecans – .25 cup
- Stevia – 1 tbsp.
- Cottage cheese – .25 cup
- Pumpkin puree – .25 cup
- Erythritol – .25 cup
- Egg yolks – 2
- Coconut or almond milk – 1 cup
- Pumpkin spice – 1 tsp.
- Xanthan gum – .25 tsp.

Preparation Method:

1. Warm a saucepan and add the butter and pecans. Cook for 8 to 10 minutes.
2. Blend the rest of the fixings in a blender
3. Add the mixture to an ice cream machine. Garnish with the pecans and serve.

Smoothie in a Bowl

Servings: 1
Macros: 4 g Net Carbs | 35 g Prot. | 35 g Fat | 570 Cal.

Ingredients:

- Almond milk – .5 cup
- Spinach – 1 cup
- Heavy cream – 2 tbsp.
- Low-carb protein powder – 1 scoop
- Coconut oil – 1 tbsp.
- Ice – 2 cubes

Ingredients for the Toppings:

- Walnuts – 4
- Raspberries – 4
- Chia seeds – 1 tsp.
- Shredded coconut – 1 tbsp.

Preparation Method:

1. Add a cup of spinach to your high-speed blender. Pour in the cream, almond milk, ice, and coconut oil.
2. Blend for a few seconds until it has an even consistency, and all ingredients are well combined. Empty the goodies into a serving dish.
3. Arrange your toppings or give them a toss and mix them together. Of course, make it pretty and alternate the strips of toppings.

Chapter 8: Delicious Smoothies

Smoothies are delicious for breakfast too!

Almond Lover Smoothie

Servings: 1 – 16 oz.

Macros: -0- g Net Carbs | 12 g Prot. | 23 g Fat | 511 Cal.

Ingredients:

- Medium banana – 1
- Almond milk – 8 oz. – 1 cup
- Plain non-fat Greek yogurt – .33 cup
- Cooked oats – .33 cup
- Almond butter – 2 tbsp.
- Almonds – 5

Preparation Method:

1. Measure all of the fixings into the cup of your NutriBullet or favorite high-speed machine.
2. Pour the milk up to the max-fill line. Blend until it is smooth and creamy.

Blackberry Cheesecake Smoothie

Servings: 1

Macros: 6.7 g Net Carbs | 6.4 g Prot. | 53 g Fat | 515 Cal.

Ingredients:

- Extra-virgin coconut oil – 1 tbsp.
- Fresh/frozen blackberries – .5 cup
- Water – .5 cup
- Coconut milk/heavy whipping cream – .25 cup
- Full-fat cream cheese or creamed coconut milk – .25 cup
- Sugar-free vanilla extract – .5 tsp.
- Liquid stevia – if desired – 3-5 drops

Preparation Method:

1. Toss all of the fixings into your blender.
2. Next, pulse until the mixture until it is smooth and frothy.
3. Add a few ice cubes and enjoy it in a chilled glass.

Blueberry – Banana Bread Smoothie

Servings: 2

Macros: 4.7 g Net Carbs | 3.1 g Prot. | 23.3 g Fat | 270 Cal.

Ingredients:

- Chia seeds – 1 tbsp.
- Golden flaxseed meal – 3 tbsp.
- Vanilla unsweetened coconut milk – 2cups
- Blueberries – .25 cup
- Liquid stevia – 10 drops
- MCT oil – 2 tbsp.
- Xanthan gum – .25 tsp.
- Banana extract – 1.5 tsp.
- Ice cubes – 2-3

Preparation Method:

1. Combine all of the ingredients into a blender.
2. Wait a few minutes for the seeds and flax to absorb some of the liquid.
3. Pulse for 1-2 minutes until well combined, and the texture you choose. Lastly, add the ice to your preference.

Blueberry – Coconut Chia Smoothie

Servings: 3

Macros: 11.3 g Net Carbs | 6.2 g Prot. | 21.1 g Fat | 249 Cal.

Ingredients:

- Coconut – .5 cup
- Unsweetened cashew or almond milk – 1 cup
- Frozen blueberries – 1 cup
- Ground chia seed – 2 tbsp.
- Full-fat Greek yogurt or almond milk – 1 cup
- Sweetener (equal to 2 tbsp. sugar) your choice
- Coconut oil – 2 tbsp.
- Optional: Cubes of ice -2-3

Preparation Method:

1. Carefully measure the ingredients and put them into your blender.
2. Mix until creamy smooth. Serve in three chilled glasses.

Blueberry & Kefir Smoothie

Servings: 2

Macros: 6.6 g Net Carbs | 3.9 g Prot. | 50 g Fat | 476 Cal.

Ingredients:

- Coconut milk kefir – 1.5 cups
- Fresh or frozen blueberries – .5 cup
- MCT oil – 2 tbsp.
- Water (+) ice cubes – .5 cup
- Sugar-free vanilla extract 1-2 tsp. or pure vanilla powder – .5 tsp.

Optional Ingredients:

- Collagen powder – 2 tbsp.
- Liquid stevia/your choice – 3-5 drops

Preparation Method:

1. Toss all of the ingredients into your blender
2. Pulse until the fixings are all mixed.
3. Serve in chilled glasses and enjoy your healthy choice!

Chocolate & Mint Smoothie

Servings: 1

Macros: 6.5 g Net Carbs | 5 g Prot. | 40 g Fat | 401 Cal.

Preparation Method:

Ingredients:

- Medium avocado – .5 of 1
- Coconut milk – .25 cup
- Unsweetened cashew/almond milk – 1 cup
- Swerve/Erythritol – 2 tbsp.
- Cocoa powder – 1 tbsp.
- Fresh mint leaves – 3-4
- MCT oil – 1 tbsp.
- Ice cubes – 2-3
- Optional: Coconut milk or whipped cream

Preparation Method:

1. Mix all of the ingredients in your blender.
2. Add ice cubes, as many as you like. Add the topping if preferred.
3. Serve and enjoy!

Chocolate Smoothie

Servings: 1 large

Macros: 4.4 g Net Carbs | 34.5 g Prot. | 46 g Fat | 570 Cal.

Ingredients:

- Large eggs – 2
- Almond or coconut butter – 1-2 tbsp.
- Extra-virgin coconut oil – 1 tbsp.
- Coconut milk or heavy whipping cream – .25 cup
- Chia seeds – 1-2 tbsp.
- Cinnamon – .5 tsp.
- Plain or chocolate whey protein – .25 cup
- Stevia extract – 3-5 drops
- Unsweetened cacao powder – 1 tbsp.
- Water – .25 cup
- Ice – .5 cup
- Vanilla extract – .5 tsp.

Preparation Method:

1. Add the eggs along with the rest of fixings into the blender.
2. Pulse until frothy. Add to a chilled glass and enjoy.

Cinnamon Roll Smoothie

Servings: 1

Macros: 0.6 g Net Carbs | 26.5 g Prot. | 3.25 g Fat | 145 Cal.

Ingredients:

- Almond milk – 1 cup
- Vanilla protein powder – 2 tbsp.
- Vanilla extract – .25 tsp.
- Cinnamon – .5 tsp.
- Sweetener – 4 tsp.
- Flax meal – 1 tsp.
- Ice – 1 cup

Preparation Method:

1. Combine all of the fixings in a blender. Add the ice last.
2. Blend on the high setting for 30 seconds until thickened.

5-Minute Mocha Smoothie

Servings: 3

Macros: 4 g Net Carbs | 3 g Prot. | 16 g Fat | 176 Cal.

Ingredients:

- Unsweetened almond milk – 1.5 cups
- Coconut milk – from the can – .5 cup
- Vanilla extract – 1 tsp.
- Instant coffee crystals – regular or decaffeinated – 1 tsp.
- Erythritol blend/granulated stevia- 3 tbsp.
- Unsweetened cocoa powder – 3 tbsp.
- Avocado – 1

Preparation Method:

1. Use a sharp knife to slice the avocado in half. Scoop the center out and discard the pit. Dice the avocado and add it along with the rest of the ingredients into the blender.
2. Mix well until smooth and serve.

Raspberry Avocado Smoothie

Servings: 2

Macros: 4 g Net Carbs | 2.5 g Prot. | 20 g Fat | 227 Cal.

Ingredients:

- Ripe avocado – 1
- Lemon juice – 3 tbsp.
- Water – 1.33 cups
- Frozen unsweetened raspberries/or choice of berries – .5 cup
- Your preference sugar equivalent – 1 tbsp. (+) 1 t.

Preparation Method:

1. Blend all of the components in a blender until creamy smooth.
2. Empty the smoothie into two chilled glasses and enjoy!

Raspberry Chocolate Cheesecake Smoothie

Servings: 1

Macros: 7 g Net Carbs | 6.9 g Prot. | 54 g Fat | 512 Cal.

Ingredients:

- Frozen or fresh raspberries – .33 cup
- Coconut milk/heavy whipping cream – .25 cup
- Full-fat cream cheese/creamed coconut milk – .25 cup
- Unsweetened cacao powder – 1 tbsp.
- Extra-virgin coconut oil – 1 tbsp.
- Water – .5 cup
- Liquid stevia extract – 3-5 drops – optional

Preparation Method:

1. Place all of the goodies for your smoothie in a blender.
2. Blend until frothy and smooth. Pour into a chilled glass and relax.

Strawberry Almond Smoothies

Servings: 2

Macros: 7 g Net Carbs | 15 g Prot. | 25 g Fat | 304 Cal.

Ingredients:

- Heavy cream – .5 cup
- Unsweetened almond milk – 16 oz.
- Stevia to taste
- Frozen unsweetened strawberries – .25 cup
- Whey vanilla isolate powder – 2 tbsp.

Preparation Method:

1. Combine each of the fixings into a blender.
2. Puree until smooth. Add a small amount of water to thin the smoothie.

Vanilla Smoothie

Servings: 1

Macros: 4 g Net Carbs | 12 g Prot. | 64 g Fat | 651 Cal.

Ingredients:

- Mascarpone full-fat cheese – .5 cup
- Large egg yolks – 2
- Water – .25 cup
- Coconut oil – 1 tbsp.
- Ice cubes – 4
- Liquid stevia 3 drops
- Pure vanilla extract – .5 tsp.
- Optional Topping: Whipped cream

Preparation Method:

1. Combine each of the ingredients in a blender until smooth.
2. Add the whipped cream for a special treat but add the carbs if any.

Conclusion

Thank you for choosing the Keto Desserts Cookbook. I hope you have enjoyed each and every recipe! The next step is to decide which tempting treat you should choose first. Just sit down and make a shopping list of all of the items you want to prepare.

Stay determined—and stand by your goals during your transition to Ketosis. Follow the instructions and recipe methods. Before long, you will be able to quickly scan other recipes and know before you finish reading how healthy they are for you and your family. Consider a few of the benefits you can achieve by following the Keto techniques:

- You will experience improved thinking skills.
- You can lower your blood pressure.
- Diabetes and prediabetes are improved using the program

The most significant benefit, though, is: *you are not hungry*.

Finally, if you found this book useful in any way, a review on Amazon is always appreciated!

Index for the Recipes

White Chocolate Bark
White Chocolate Pecan Halves

Delicious Fat Bombs

Allspice Almond Fat Bombs
Almond Butter Fat Bombs
Almond – Choco Fat Bombs
Blackberry Coconut Fat Bombs
Blueberry Cream Cheese Fat Bombs
Bulletproof Fat Bombs
Cacao Coconut Fat Bombs
Chocolate Fat Bombs
Chocolate Peanut Butter Fat Bombs
Chocolate Peppermint Fat Bombs
Coconut Macaroons Fat Bombs
Coffee Fat Bombs
Craving Buster Fat Bombs
Dark Chocolate Fat Bombs
Dark Chocolate Raspberry Fat Bombs
Lemonade Fat Bombs
Maple Almond Fudge Fat Bombs
Pistachio & Almond Fat Bombs
Raspberry Coconut Bark Fat Bombs
Stuffed Pecan Fat Bomb

Chapter 3: Cookies Galore

Amaretti Cookies
Chocolate Cookies
Chocolate Chip Cookies
Chocolate Coconut Cookies
Chocolate-Filled Peanut Butter Cookies
Chocolate Macaroon Cookies with Coconut
Coconut Almond Cookies

Coconut – No-Bake Cookies
Cream Cheese Cookies
Ginger Snap Cookies
Nut Butter Cookies
Orange Walnut Cookies
P B & J Cookies
Peanut Butter Cookies
Strawberry Thumbprints

Chapter 4: Bar Cookies

Almond Pumpkin Seed Bars
Cheesecake Mocha Bars
Chia Bars
Coconut Cashew Protein Bars – No-Bake
Coconut Chia Bars
Coconut Cream Brownies
Dark Chocolate Brownies
Easy Brownie in a Mug
Peanut Butter Protein Bars
Pumpkin Bars with Cream Cheese Frosting
Tart Lemon-Lime Bars

Chapter 5: Cakes & Cheesecakes

Cakes

Berries & Cream Keto Cake with Brown Sugar Whipped Cream
Chocolate Lava Cake
Chocolate Roll Cake
Gingerbread – Slow Cooker
Lemon Cake
Mocha Pudding Cake – Slow Cooker
Pumpkin Blondies
Raspberry Coconut Cake – Slow Cooker

Chocolate Ice Cream
Chocolate Shakes
Mint Chocolate Chip Shake
Peanut Butter Caramel Milkshake
Pudding Pops
Pumpkin Ice Cream
Smoothie in a Bowl

Chapter 8: Delicious Smoothies

Almond Lover Smoothie
Blackberry Cheesecake Smoothie
Blueberry Banana Smoothie
Blueberry Coconut Chia Smoothie
Blueberry & Kefir Smoothie
Chocolate Mint Smoothie
Chocolate Smoothie
Cinnamon Roll Smoothie
5-Minute Smoothie
Raspberry & Avocado Smoothie
Raspberry Chocolate Cheesecake Smoothie
Strawberry Almond Smoothies
Vanilla Smoothie

Made in the USA
Lexington, KY
21 June 2019